When The Lion Roars

*A Devotional
to the Egyptian Goddess
Sekhmet*

Compiled by Galina Krasskova

When The Lion Roars

A Devotional to the Egyptian Goddess Sekhmet

Compiled by Galina Krasskova

Asphodel Press

Hubbardston, Massachusetts

Asphodel Press
12 Simond Hill Road
Hubbardston, MA 01452

When The Lion Roars: A Devotional to the Egyptian Goddess
Sekhmet
© 2011 by Galina Krasskova
ISBN 978-0-9825798-7-9

Printed in cooperation with
Lulu Enterprises, Inc.
860 Aviation Parkway, Suite 300
Morrisville, NC 27560

For Sekhmet.

And for Rev. Queen Mother Imakhu, Kemetic Elder priestess, magnificent water woman and fierce warrior. Our meeting was a gift from Sekhmet, one for which I shall ever be grateful. Thank you for your work and your gracious blessings. May Sekhmet ever smile upon you and your House. Ashe! Ashe! Ashe!

A very special thank you to Mary Ann Glass for providing the photos for the cover montage, and to K.C. Hulsman for designing the cover.

Sekhmet by Rebecca Vander Jagt

Contents

Rituals and Meditations

Recipes

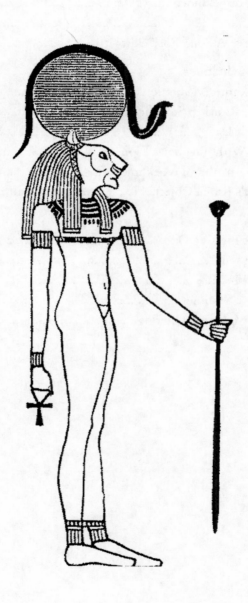

Foreword: Sekhmet As Mentor

Sekhmet has been an important part of my spiritual life since I was 19. She was the first Goddess—indeed, the first Deity—with Whom I felt any type of deep connection. She spoke for me, and as I progressed in my devotion and dedication, She claimed me. I was Her priest before I ever consciously became Odin's, and it was through Her that I learned the protocols of devotion. In time, of course, She broke me down, built me up and passed me on, and I was given to the Gods of my ancestors. I was given to Loki and, eventually, Odin, who owns me as I love Him: utterly. I would have it no other way. That was later, though, by several years. First there was Sekhmet, and all the ways in which She opened me up to Her fire.

She first came for me in 1991, and I was fortunate shortly thereafter to find a group of devoted women in the Fellowship of Isis, who helped me to temper the press of Her fire with the practicalities of learning how best to honor Her (and other Deities as well). After several years of work – and I hope, growth – I was initiated, then ordained in 1995 as Her priest, also through the Fellowship of Isis. Though I am Heathen and now both a *gythia* and a shaman, I cherish that ordination. I cherish that connection to Her, even as memories of the ways in which She readied me for service still occasionally leave me shaking. Sekhmet is not an easy teacher. I do not think it an exaggeration to say that She prepared me for service to Odin. She set my feet securely on the path of that service and taught me the discipline necessary to thrive and serve well. That is no small thing at all, and even now I often find myself overcome with gratitude. She was a harsh teacher, but I was an undisciplined whelp determined to walk the warrior's path, in desperate need of self-control and training. I needed Her harshness. Where I was sometimes unfocused, She was implacable. Where I was often afraid, She breathed the fire of Her courage into my heart. She not only brought me home to my Gods, She brought me home to myself. She took me in hand and, as popular vernacular might put it, "schooled" me in many ways necessary for the work that I now do. I'm grateful, immensely grateful, and while I am now owned by Odin, I still consider Her to be my spiritual Mother.

This devotional should come as no surprise, then, though I'm sure a great many Heathens will likely be shaking their heads in confusion or derision, wondering what on earth I'm doing writing for an Egyptian Deity. Sekhmet was good to me, in ways that even now move me immensely to consider. This devotional is a gift of gratitude. It is the acknowledgement of a debt that I doubt I shall ever be able to repay. Sekhmet made me a priest, and it was the priest who was later transformed into a *godatheow* (god-slave) and shaman. She taught me to bow my head before the Gods. She taught me the foolish impotence of my arrogance. She taught me humility, and how to stand in the presence of the holy without fleeing in terror. She taught me to meet obstacles without hesitation. She taught me how to be useful, and most of all, She taught me to find tremendous joy in service.

So to those for whom gratitude is an alien concept, I have nothing to say. My words are not for you. To those who understand the deep impact a God or Goddess can have on one's life, who hunger for it, and who cherish those moments, for whom gratitude is a way of life, I offer these pages in exaltation of the Goddess Sekhmet. For those who have not honored Sekhmet at all, who simply do not know Her, I hope that these words, from many of Her devotees across the globe, will serve to ignite a hunger for Her presence that nothing but the sweet discipline of devotion may quench. Sekhmet is a Force that nothing may surpass, least of all our quailing, aching, hungry human hearts.

It has been a joy over this past year networking with many of Her devotees and slowly compiling the book that you now hold in your hands. In many respects, it has steeped me once more in the fire of Her presence. I hope it will do the same for each person who reads it. That is my wish: that all those who read this may be opened in some way to Her fire and the transformation that it brings. So read with care and prepare yourself: She is a force that cannot and will not be denied.

May Sekhmet bless you with Her fire.

GALINA KRASSKOVA
CONOWINGO, MD
JULY 30, 2011

Articles and Essays

Devotion Is A Warrior's Art
Galina Krasskova

In the desert of my heart You came.
Lady of fire, You stripped me bare.
With fire and searing heat You opened me,
Implacable One.
Mighty Warrior Goddess,
You have devoured me,
torn the flesh from my the withered reliquary of my heart,,
gnawed at the battered bones of my spirit.
You have nourished Yourself on my pain
until I could not run,
could not flee,
could not beg, or plead, or cry.
And in doing so,
You have gifted me
with wholeness.

> *"The dance of battle is always played to the same*
> *impatient rhythm. What begins in a surge of violent*
> *motion is always reduced to the perfectly still."*
> *-Sun Tzu*

I have always been attracted to the warrior arts. It is a deeply ingrained passion that has honed me and honed my spirituality over the years. Picking up a sword for the first time, when I began my study of Iaido as an adult, was like coming home. Closing my hands around a Glock 9mm when first learning to shoot, even more so. There is a peace in the warrior's abode, a calm serenity unexpected and unsought after, that comes as a natural consequence of the discipline and intensely powerful focus needed for mastery of these arts. Not for me the Maiden, Mother, or Crone. No, when I became Pagan I instinctively knew myself to be drawn to a far different type of Goddess.

From the very beginning, I sought out Warrior Goddesses: Sekhmet, Kali, Morrigan—Goddesses who revel in the bringing of death at weapon's edge, at conquering the knife-edge terror of impending mortality, of tempering the chaotic playground of one's emotions, and of living a life of single-minded purpose. I was drawn to Goddesses who understood violence and the unrelenting mastery of it. Of course, in those days—easily 15 years ago—no one in Modern Paganism really spoke of the war-Goddesses. It was a *verboten* subject, as though the path of the warrior was diametrically opposed to any spiritual path at all. For me, it was never so. For me, it was an ongoing path of harsh clarity. Of course, I learned very early on that not everything that is harsh is bad.

I was taken up by Sekhmet very early on in my Fellowship of Isis days, finally becoming Her priestess. Eventually, She led me to Odin and Loki and handed over the reins, but even so, She will always and forever remain my Mother. Her lessons were harsh and Her training implacable. In many respects, She readied me not only for Odin but for the work that He would have me do. She made me a warrior, broke and honed me, and I emerged the better for it. Every night for a year, I prayed to Sekhmet. I prayed for Her to burn me, purify me, strip me of everything that might interfere with my spirituality. I prayed for Her to make of me the most useful of tools. (That is a secret most warriors won't think to tell. The highest compliment we can give or receive is this: to say one has been of use). She took me at my word. I discovered rather quickly that it is one thing to pray to a Goddess or God, and another to be answered. There is no necessary responsibility in the mere utterance of words. There is hope. There is wishing. There may be commitment, but if one's prayer is not immediately answered, it is easy enough to back away safely, secure in one's own world. But when one receives a definite answer, that entire world shatters. Nothing is ever the same again.

Sekhmet destroyed me.

She took an impulsive child and stripped me bare. She made of that child a devotee and a priest. She readied my heart for devotion, for service, for love. She took from me my profession, my apartment, my friends and spiritual guides. She left me barren and bereft and anguished—and I am grateful. She took me to a place of desolation so profound that I had only Her to sustain me, only Her to turn to. I needed that. I needed to be reduced to simplicity, humility, and raw, unhoned desire. I needed to be broken.

I served Sekhmet for many years. To this day, I pay homage to Her for setting my feet upon a warrior's path, for naming those things I knew lay within me, for giving me the courage to live as She wished. Those things I learned at Her feet prepared me not only for priesthood, but for a life of centered devotion. Of all the gifts I learned, both from Goddesses of war and my study of warrior arts, the most invaluable one was this: when I chose to commit to my Gods, I did so fully. When I set my feet upon the path that eventually led me to become inextricably bound to Woden—as my life now is—She had already prepared me for the commitment.

Ah, Sekhmet seemed so cruel at the time. I, who had played at being a warrior for so long, who had hungered for the starkness of the training, learned soon enough what it meant to belong to such a Goddess. The compassion of a Warrior Goddess is the most ruthless compassion of all. It leaves no room for emotion or sentiment, no room for doubt or fear or regret. All of these things must be sacrificed. All of these things are given over to the duty of unending *puja*.

From Sekhmet, I learned the value of conflict. I learned that within me at my deepest core lay a beast of rage and fury, a killer that would devour all I held dear in my life, if I let it. Oh, I had a temper. I still do, though I strive hard not to give it free rein. My rage would boil up in word and deed eating away at my integrity, reputation, and friendships. No one else could calm that beast. It was for me rein it in, and that was a duty at which I was failing. I saw myself in the mirror of Her fire as I never hope to see myself again. She shattered me in that first year, and then slowly began the process of rebuilding. Looking back, I realize that She was giving me exactly what I needed. She was tempering me like a blade is tempered in the heated forge—being beaten, hammered, molded, and beaten again, subjected to annealing flame over and over again. I'm afraid I was very stubborn, and it took me a very long time to fully accept the precious gift of self-discipline that She offered.

Eventually, I learned to rule (at least a little more) that beast of rage that lay inside. I had a vicious temper, along with a physicality and training enough to be dangerous, but I learned restraint. I was deeply passionate about everything I did for good or for ill, but I learned to govern my passions. I learned to examine emotions carefully and then to set them aside. "A warrior acts from duty first," She taught me, "and she does not fear to live." There are no façades with these Goddesses, no room for sentiment, no hiding from truths, however painful. Most of all, there is no safety. She, and She alone, taught me to love my Gods without condition, to step into the fire of ecstasy and inspiration that They bring, and willingly court immolation. It was the Warrior who made of me a mystic.

I learned to pray with a sword in my hand—or a gun, for I find pistol shooting to be extremely calming and meditative. It is ice to the heat of the sword's song. I learned through strict training to seek an unerring center, to allow nothing to deter me from my goals—not my own ego, my own stubborn resistance to change, my own laziness, my emotional upset, and certainly not anyone or anything outside of myself. I learned to seek the Gods with an unswerving surety that scares even me when I think back on it. She made sure I would never be a slave to my own fear, my own desires, my own pride, ego, or hubris.

I was painfully young when I came to Her, and hungry for knowledge. Sekhmet pushed me pretty quickly into serious study of the martial arts. This, of course, was no hardship. My only difficulty lay in deciding what to study! Of all the weapons in the world, the *katana* has always held the greatest fascination for me. It presents clean, almost stark lines, and must be wielded with a ruthless precision that causes my spirit to rejoice. After observing one class at a local dojo, I knew that I had found the martial art for me. The only exhilaration comparable was the moment, a few years later, when I learned to shoot a gun. Through the years the Gods used my study of Iaido as a very visible parallel to my spiritual health. My work in the dojo came to reflect, sometimes to frightening proportions, the work that I was doing spiritually and what progress (or not) I was making.

Best of all, at the dojo, my aggressive nature is considered a virtue, though one in need of direction, which the physical discipline of training itself provided. During the very first class I took, on one of the hottest days of summer, I nearly passed out. I truly thought I was going to die. But one adapts, and a little pain is good for the spirit.

It is an uncomfortable thing, however, this process of stripping away. For that is what I have committed, by virtue of my commitment to my Gods, to continually doing. When I entered the dojo, I was taken back to the beginning and forced to gain those skills and self-control that I should have been trained in years ago, well before I ever became an adult. I was a child again, fumbling for understanding. My meditation and magic came to lie on the material plane, in a stark training hall and endless repetition of *kata*, my ritual garb was *hakama* and *gi*, and my libations sweat, bloody hands, and aching muscles. (Those initial classes during the summer proved the first time in my life where I've been so sore I just sat down at home and cried.) This was all to Sekhmet's liking. When She relinquished Her hold on me, passing me into the arms and auspices of Woden (a God known for His penchant for strong women), I was a completely different creature than the one that had first reached out for the Gods.

Through Her, I had been forged into something, someone that could be of service to the God that I love beyond breath and being. I fell deeply in love with Woden, and service to Him soon began to govern my life. To love a God so deeply that you willingly seek out the sharing of Their pain requires a will strong enough to endure proximity with the terrifying reality of the numinous. It requires a will and a sense of self forged in stone, one that will not break under the weight of duty, nor seek the safety of imagination and personal comfort. I have many faults (my temper, for one, remains a constant reminder that I am far from perfect), but there is one small thing I have learned as only a warrior can: when there is nothing else to be done, in the midst of the most tumultuous of storms, hold fast and endure. I like to hope that this one quality has enabled me to be of some use to Woden and the other Gods that I adore. At the very least, I think it ensures I am not too much of a burden.

Warriorship is not a metaphor for me. It remains incomprehensible to me that one could grow on a spiritual-warrior path without ever exploring and embracing the qualities traditionally associated with warriorship. In my life, both daily and devotional, they remain foundational, however disturbing that may be in these politically correct times. Walking this path has enabled me to grow in devotion, love, and commitment to my Gods. It has impacted the ways in which I relate to the world, and the ways in which I serve my Gods. It has made me a better person. I owe that to Sekhmet.

Sekhmet
Edward Butler

Sekhmet (Sakhmet, Sachmet or -mis, etc.), whose name means "the Powerful", is depicted as a lioness-headed woman, often with the solar disk atop her head. A Goddess of healing and of pestilence alike, Sekhmet often bears the epithet "Eye of Re", identifying her as the executor (*irt*, "eye" can also be read as *ir.t*, "doer" or "agent") of the will of the sovereign solar power of the cosmos. Sekhmet and Hathor both operate as the "Eye of Re" in the myth from the *Book of the Celestial Cow* in which Re sends first Hathor, then Sekhmet to strike rebellious humanity. Sekhmet is to "wade in their blood as far as Herakleopolis [Hnes]," on a southward path (referring to the southward course of the sun after the summer solstice). Re saves humanity by ordering the production of a great quantity of beer with an additive to make it red like blood, with which the Goddess is intoxicated and her destructive mission terminated, perhaps at Kom el-Hisn in the Western Delta. Sekhmet can cause, as well as avert, all forms of pestilence, whether natural disaster, famine, or epidemic, but she is particularly associated with illness and its cure, and priests of Sekhmet played a prominent role in Egyptian medicine. Sekhmet's consort is Ptah, and she is the mother of Nefertum.

Sekhmet's "arrows" (often specified as seven in number) are a common term for her striking power, as is her "knife" and her "flame". Several spells exist (nos. 13-15, 20 in Borghouts) which are designed to protect against pestilence associated with the transition into the New Year. Hence the title of no. 13 in Borghouts, *The Book of the Last Day of the Year*, which make frequent mention of Sekhmet and of the demons in her retinue, her "emissaries" (*wepwety*), "wanderers" (*shemayu*), or "murderers" (*khayti*), who must

Quoted from:
http://henadology.wordpress.com/theology/netjeru/sekhmet/
Used with permission.

be placated. In many of these spells, it seems that Sekhmet's protection is won by identifying the individual with Horus—as in no. 20: "I am your Horus, Sekhmet." Horus is also often called "sprout of Sekhmet" in such spells, in which the word translated as "sprout" is *wadj*—Horus is thus literally the "greening" of the Goddess, who is paradigmatically red with blood (note that the papyrus scepter which Sekhmet and a number of other Goddesses carry is also *wadj*). The relationship between Sekhmet and Horus is not one of parentage, but rather alludes to Sekhmet being one of the wrathful Goddesses charged with the protection of Horus during his vulnerable infancy in the marshes. The pharaoh is sometimes characterized as "brother [*sen*]/image [*senen*] of Nefertum, born of Sekhmet." State rituals involving Sekhmet were particularly important at the New Year, which was linked to the heliacal rising of Sirius, and thus took place in late summer (northern hemisphere). The purpose of such rituals appears to have been to prevent the contamination of the new year by inimical forces emanating from the old year, as well as to ensure the proper alignment of life on earth with its divine paradigms. Hence, two of the most important rituals involving Sekhmet at this time were known as the "union of the disk," focusing on the physical disk of the sun, the *aten*, and the "conferring of the heritage." It is important to note that the term *iadet*, or "pestilence," which is associated with Sekhmet, is a very broad term, and appears to be identical to a word for "net," which occurs repeatedly in spells from the afterlife literature to protect the soul from becoming trapped like a fish in such "nets" (e.g., *Coffin Texts* spells 473-481). Sekhmet can thus be regarded as having power over virtually any misfortune or "net" of circumstances which might "trap" the individual indiscriminately.

Sekhmet is often paired or juxtaposed with Wadjet, who also bears the title "Eye of Re," as in *CT* spell 757, where the operator affirms, "My White Crown is Sekhmet, my Red Crown is Wadjet," referring to the crowns of Upper and Lower Egypt, in accord with a tendency in Egyptian thought to identify defenders of the crown, such as Sekhmet and Wadjet, with the crown itself. In a version of the "Opening of the Mouth" ceremony (*BD* spell 23), the deceased, whose *ka* statue has been empowered, states, "I am Sekhmet-Wadjet who dwells in the west of heaven." In a ritual for offering meat to the sacred hawk that lived at the temple of Horus at Edfu, in which we probably see an adaptation of a ritual performed originally on behalf of the king, we find the interesting invocation, "O Sekhmet of yesterday, Wadjet of today, thou hast come and hast replenished this table of the Living Falcon ... even as thou didst for thy father Horus, when thou camest forth from Pe," (Blackman, p. 60 [155, 8-9]). Sekhmet replenishes the table inasmuch as meat-offerings are identified with the flesh of royal foes, with the text's invocation of Sekhmet turning the occasion of the meal into an enactment of the destruction of the king's enemies. The identification of Sekhmet with "yesterday" and Wadjet with "today" is unusual and harder to explain, but it perhaps invokes Sekhmet's protection against the nonbeing of the past. In *CT* spell 957, Sekhmet is juxtaposed with Nekhbet, the operator affirming, "I have ascended to the upper sky, and I have fashioned Nekhbet; I have descended to the lower sky of Re, and I have fashioned Sekhmet." Another sort of opposition is posed in the *Book of the Celestial Cow*, in which Hathor is sent to strike humans in the mountains or desert, while Sekhmet is sent to strike them in the Delta.

Multiplication seems in some fashion essential to Sekhmet, perhaps because power diversifies itself at its points of application; thus she is referred to as "Sekhmet of multiple appearances," (*Edfou* I, 278 & IV, 116) and as "Sekhmet the great, mistress of the Sekhmets," (*Edfou* VII, 14). In the Tenth Hour of the *Amduat* book, the healing of the *wedjat*, the Eye of Horus, is shown being carried out by Thoth, in baboon form, and eight forms of Sekhmet, four with lioness heads and four with human heads.

References:

Allen, T. G. 1974. *The Book of the Dead or Going Forth by Day*.
   Chicago: University of Chicago Press. [*BD*]

Blackman, A. M. 1945. "The King of Egypt's Grace Before Meat."
   Journal of Egyptian Archaeology 31: 57-73.

Borghouts, J. F. 1978. *Ancient Egyptian Magical Texts*. Leiden: E. J.
   Brill.

Faulkner, R. O. 1973-8. *The Ancient Egyptian Coffin Texts*. 3 vols.
   Warminster: Aris & Phillips Ltd. [*CT*]

The Roar Of Desert Winds In The City
K.C. Hulsman

Life takes us on unexpected roads, and the journey is often full of twists and turns we may not have seen coming. Years ago, like so many other Pagans, I had been not only Christian, but a devout born-again Baptist. My path led me unexpectedly to Paganism, and while this would eventually lead me to Heathenry, the transition had its share of rough roads to traverse, and some unexpected landmarks to visit along the way.

Not too long after I was a newly converted Pagan, I was making my very first trip to New York City to visit a friend who lived in the area. She, of course, played the gracious host, shuttling me around the city and showing me the sites. When she first told me we were going to the Metropolitan Museum of Art, I was thrilled. Every since I was a young child, I have loved going to museums, and some of my fondest memories are connected with them. Even today, I trek out a few times a year to take advantage of some of the amazing exhibits in my area.

As we headed out that cold December day to the museum, I knew there was something "special" that my friend wanted to show me, but with mischief in her eyes she wouldn't tell me what. So I settled myself into a wait, and thankfully I only had to wait a couple of hours, so it was bearable.

Processing through the museum and gaining our admission tags for the day, we set out through labyrinthine mazes of art and sculpture. We passed through the Asian art galleries, some of the Greek and Roman collection, and then wound our way through the vast complex of galleries focused on ancient Egypt, from the Paleolithic era up to the Roman era. There were lovely examples of faience art, small idols of the Egyptian Gods and Goddesses, canopic jars, a vast array of jewelry, and other common items in the museum's many display cases. Everywhere in the museum, even with the heat running and the body heat emanating from the crowded throng, it had been just a little bit on the chilly side for me personally. But as we slowly moved throughout the Egyptian galleries, I began feeling first warm, then flushed, and then like I was burning up with a fever. I removed my winter coat and draped it over my arm. Then I removed my sweater and draped it over my coat, which left me in a lightweight knit top. Still I was hot, and I pushed my sleeves up. Unfortunately, I couldn't remove anything else unless I wanted to flash people with my bra, and I am a bit too shy for that. Around me other people looked at me like I was crazy, as they shivered in their coats from the chill wintry day.

Then I turned the corner.

I heard a roar in my ears as a sudden rush of blood went coursing through my veins. I felt as if I had been suddenly blasted with the heat of some unseen furnace as a desert wind only I could feel passed through me, making me tingle from head to toe. I glimpsed just beyond the open archway to my right side a seated depiction of the Goddess Sekhmet in stone. Beside Her were several other identical images in dark basalt.

I lost a few seconds of time standing there in awe, thunderstruck, feeling the presence of the Goddess Sekhmet most strongly around me. Somehow, I had found myself in an unexpected holy place in the heart not only of New York, but inside one of the most famous museums in the world. Slowly, as though a fog had lifted from my mind, awareness of the ordinary, mundane world around me returned, and I stepped out of the way of the museum patrons ushering in and out of the room. I saw that knowledgeable glint in my friend's eye as she eagerly took in my reaction. This was apparently the surprise she'd had in mind on our outing to the Met.

These statues are not just mere physical representations of a great Goddess, but are charged holy relics that are more than 3000 years old. They were once danced to, anointed, and worshipped daily for untold years by the ancient Egyptian believers. These statues are dated by the museum to be from the reign of Amenhotep III, ca. 1390-1352 B.C., and originally came from the Temple of Mut at Karnak where hundreds of these statues sat in long rows together. They are pieces of devotional iconography redolent with the power of Her presence. They come from a time before we had forgotten how to honor the Gods and ancestors.

Feeling dwarfed like a child by an adult, I looked up into the carved face of the Goddess in wonder, and words of praise and prayer fell quietly as a joyful mantra from my lips. Here was The Eternally Burning One, Her presence palpable like the heat that radiates off of sun-warmed stone. Slowly I walked from one depiction of the Lion-Headed Goddess Sekhmet to the next, and then reaching the end of a series of Her icons, I turned to look across a reflecting pool representing the great Nile, to find in the same room the transplanted Temple of Dendur dedicated to Isis, Osiris, and two deified sons of a local chieftain (Pediese, Pihor). It had been saved from Egypt before its original location was flooded during the building of the Aswan High Dam in the 1960s.

Those familiar with Egyptian belief will know that Sekhmet is connected with the Goddess of Justice, Ma'at, who stands in Osiris' Hall of Judgment. To have these holy statues of Her present in a room housing a transplanted temple with ties to Osiris surely must reinforce the sacred connection that can be found at this site, for those who make the journey to visit it and are open to Her.

As I continued around the room, exploring the temple and other Egyptian artifacts on display, I was still feeling quite feverish, while those around me continued to look at me like I was crazy as they shivered in the big drafty room that overlooked a snowy and slush-drizzled Central Park. After making one last walk past the processional of Sekhmet statues, I bid Her adieu and left the wing. A few rooms over, the flushed feeling left, and then I was cold, and re-layered my sweater and coat back on.

Through the years, I have heard of others who have had their own encounters with the Goddess here. As someone who lives across the country, I make it a point to try to go by and say hello to this Goddess when I find myself in Her neighborhood on my various visits to New York. While subsequent trips never quite rendered as potent as an experience as that first time, they are always worthwhile to me.

While the installation is treated merely as a special collection of artifacts in a museum, and not given the sort of sacred deference it is (in my opinion) due, it is still a hidden gem where Her presence can be found and is accessible to those unable to journey to Egypt's ancient sites. Of course, She can always be found in prayers, but there is something very extraordinary about connecting with such ancient hallowed relics. So if you find yourself in New York, you should pay your respects to the Goddess Sekhmet, She who is a giver of joys and ecstasies, and perhaps you may have your own special tale to take away from the pilgrimage.

Consumed By The Lion
Shin Cynikos

In the Centre Street Building of the Walters Art Museum, on the second floor, I found myself flanked by two massive three-thousand-pound statues of Sekhmet. Each of them sat on a white pedestal on either side of the entrance to the "Ancient World" wing of the museum. Somehow I was drawn to the one to the right of me, with the solar disk over her head. I shifted position slightly onto my left leg, to alleviate the dull throbbing in my hip which seemed to keep pace with the throbbing in my skull. Lyme disease had decided to move in with me and take up shop, wearing down my defenses, and for the first time, leaving me faced with the possibility of life with chronic pain. This was something that, at the time, I was not eager to accept. Chronic illness was something that happened to other people. It wouldn't happen to me. It couldn't. My stubbornness in part defined my very nature. I frequently overtaxed myself, frequently ignored the signals my body was sending me. Inevitably, as I struggled against it, it only made things worse.

I looked left and right. The hall was relatively quiet and empty. I began to approach the statue, forcing myself to walk normally so as to not attract attention to my pain. I stared up at her face. She seemed so peaceful and serene, sitting there. It was almost disarming. A goddess of war. A torturer extraordinaire. *Lady of Slaughter*, they called her. Looking at her, she seemed anything but. Sitting with her hands in her lap, she seemed almost meditative, calm. I knew her also to be a goddess of healing; her priests synonymous with doctors, she was the giver and curer of disease and illness. That's why I approached her, then. That was why I needed her. In a way, because of what I knew then, I even blamed her for my illness. "You did this to me," I thought. "Now take it away."

I held my breath. I drew closer, sensing an electricity in the air. I hesitated for what seemed to be a fraction of a second, holding my breath. I moved forward again, and before I knew it, I was standing directly beside her pillar, close enough to touch her. I sat down beside her. I was so close. Her statue was old, so old, and it radiated an immense power, like a battery. Beyond her lay more artifacts, more mysteries. It's why I come to museums. They are my temples, my places of worship. I go there to find peace, to find unity. Closing my eyes, I can hear their whispers. The artifacts and relics speak from across the vast stretches of time. I sit among them, and listen to their stories. They are so eager to tell their stories, and I am eager to listen.

Everything was so still, so quiet. If not for that uneasy feeling, that sensation of electricity in the air right before a gathering storm, I would have chastised myself for being so hesitant. I forgot then, that when a big cat, such as a lion, stalks its prey, it will stay perfectly still, frozen like a statue, crouched in the bush. In the moment before the pounce, the whole savannah seems to hold its breath. Then I did it. What did I do exactly? I touched her. I would like to state for the record that this is a big no-no, and really, I knew better. The acids, oils, and salts on human skin can damage artifacts—even stone ones. Even still, I took my index finger, rubbed it generously on my pants leg (as if that would make any difference), and touched it to her old stone feet. Comparatively, it was like touching an electric socket. And really, that was all it took, in the beginning.

The years and months since then were interesting times, with repeated bouts of illness and increased frequency of migraines (one of which caused me to pass out, and ended me up in the hospital). I was haunted by dreams of getting torn apart by big cats—bones snapping, tendons ripping, blood spilling onto the land. They were large, female predators; lions, leopards and cheetahs. They were bigger than their physical counterparts, each crowned with the halo of the sun. My migraine auras and visions were intense. Every time, I felt as if my skull was being crushed in the jaws of a vast predator, or perhaps I was being suffocated, or stabbed in the eye by an ibis, or vulture. They came in and out of my dreams, speaking in many voices, rippling against a backdrop of a blood-red sun. But she was there. Always, she was there. Sekhmet.

Gradually, I grew stronger. The pain was brought under control, the bouts with illness less frequent, less lingering. This did not come without a price. Every bout of pain was a fight, win or lose, it was all me. But I fought. I chose to fight instead of simply letting it control me. She wouldn't let me lay down and die. In a pride of lions, a lion that just gives up is a dead lion, as the pride cannot afford to sustain a weak link. So I fought. I learned breathing exercises to control the pain. I learned how to harness the violent power of my migraines to take me on fascinating and terrifying journeys, both to the deeper workings of my soul, and to the outer limits of the Otherworlds. She taught me that pain does not solely define who I am, nor do any of my past struggles. They don't define me any more than my internal female organs and XX-chromosomes identify me as a female. I am a man, a very androgynous man, but still a man. And Sekhmet, as the Red Lady of the menstrual cycle, had much to teach me about that, too—that my manhood isn't stripped because of the body I inhabit. That I can use this sacred in-betweenness as a powerful and transformative tool.

Other things began to happen in my life. My father went twice to Afghanistan with the Air Force, an experience that changed him, and really, changed the whole family. It helped me become more aware of the warriors in my life, such as my grandfathers, and a very close and dear friend of the family who was formerly in Special Ops. I started to volunteer for a nonprofit organization that sends care packages to individual soldiers overseas. Out of an arbitrary list of names from this mostly Christian group, I was first assigned to a Heathen man serving as a medic in Afghanistan. Despite the high stress of his job, he always wrote me regularly, and we kept in touch through this correspondence for quite some time. I still have all of the letters he has sent me, tucked between the paws of Wepwawet on my primary altar. The experience changed me a lot, and I learned so much from this man in that short period of correspondence. It was definitely a character-building exercise, in that it brought the focus away from my own problems and onto the needs of others, and helped refocus the meanings of the words "courage" and "honor". And even words like sadness, pain, and loss.

Sometimes the best lessons learned are on the end of a lion's paw. What I wanted was for someone to just take all those struggles away from me, to just make everything better. But Sekhmet doesn't do that. She is a very harsh teacher, as most lion-mothers are. But these teachings build strong and sturdy cubs, who grow into adults that have to tangle with animals several times their own size and body weight. And really, if one observes a pride of lions, it is the females that get things done. That's what Sekhmet is all about. She won't come to you with a magic wand to take all of your troubles away. She will come, teeth bared and claws unsheathed. She will rip you to shreds and rebuild you from the ground up, if necessary. Sometimes that is what is needed. She is a Lady of many epithets, but she is also the personification of Lion, and the personification of the burning ray of the Sun that destroys all as well as nurtures all. She teaches, above all other things, that you cannot have creation without destruction. A sometimes harsh lesson, which she beats out in the wild red dance of the desert.

Mine Is A Heart of Carnelian: Lessons From A Mother To A Daughter
Melitta Benu

Before I began working with Persephone, before I began working with Hekate, I served the goddess Sekhmet. I was nineteen years old and just beginning to take a very serious look at why I kept flirting with Paganism, despite the fact that I had been a practicing (then lapsed) Catholic before that. I was experimenting with Wicca, and some ceremonial magick, and was taking classes in Zen meditation, as well as a class about the "Science of Being" (developed by Baron Eugene Fersen) given by Lady Mimi of Esoterica Occult Goods in New Orleans.[1] Many of these experiences were serving to shake the bonds of my former religious life from me, and while they were broadening my horizons, I missed the experience of a close, devotional bond with divinity. I wasn't willing to adhere to Christianity anymore (though I was not averse to others doing so), but I wasn't sure where to go from where I was. Then, during a party thrown by Esoterica, I met with a group of people who introduced me to Egyptian reconstructionist religion. And Sekhmet.

Since then, Sekhmet has been my mother. No, I don't mean "mother" in the delusional way, and no, I'm not claiming divine parentage. When I say this, I speak as someone who grew up without a much of a mother figure, and the relationship I had (and still have) with Sekhmet fills this role in my life—when the pains of life shook me and I was brought to my knees, time and again, as we all are, I would turn to Sekhmet for strength. Rather than being the mother who coddles and enables, She was the mother who taught me to look pain in the eye and laugh. Though She extended Her hand and Her strength, to me, She also taught me how to use my own strength to stand on my own. It was Sekhmet who taught me that pain and hardship can be a tool, and to understand myself, and

---

[1] Those of you in the New Orleans area, you don't want to miss Esoterica or the fabulous Lady Mimi.

my spiritual self, as a sword which is hammered and fired to become something stronger than it was. And, when I was at the end of that strength and unable to continue, Sekhmet was the one I felt extending to me a boundless sense of love, protectiveness, and pride, in much the same way a mother lioness protects and comforts her cubs.

As well, a mother lioness tries to teach her cubs the necessary skills they need to survive. In the same vein, Sekhmet has also taught me, through experience shared with Her, lessons that have become integral to the way I live my life. I have chosen five that I am most comfortable sharing.

Strength is earned and comes through effort.

Just as our physical muscles are not at their strongest without a conscious effort to exercise them, the same goes for our internal strength, which grows through our choices and our trials. While a certain amount of inner strength may come easier for some than others, it is through the conscious application of one's will and the exercise of one's integrity that one truly develops this strength. Sekhmet, as a goddess of war and battle, knows that it is tests of will and inner fortitude that forge a whole human being- our hardships form us, our joys normalize us[2], and the lessons we learn from both sharpen us into a weapon of great power. But we must put forth the effort to correctly interpret and channel these experiences, because if not, the hammer which could form us may break us, the joys that normalize us could make us weak, and the lessons which sharpen us could pass us by, leaving us dull and perhaps even feeble. The work, any work, does not do itself—we must take the initiative.

---

[2] "Normalize" is meant in the way of heating and cooling a sword, which removes stresses in the blade.

Strength is in accepting your vulnerabilities, not denying them.

A person who denies their vulnerabilities falls prey to them— this, itself, was a very hard lesson for me to learn. Sometimes, vulnerabilities come with a certain amount of shame or guilt, especially if the vulnerability is something that is culturally taboo or if, because of your vulnerability, you have been taken advantage of in some way. And yet, in accepting our vulnerabilities and seeing them for what they are, we learn to turn them into strengths. Our weaknesses are meant to teach us, and there are ways to find the proverbial diamonds in the dung heap—it just takes, again, effort and the consistent application of one's will. Sekhmet taught me, through a lot of trial and error, to embrace myself along with all my flaws, and miraculously, I've learned to turn some of them into tools for me to use in my own life's journey—something I never thought I'd be able to do. As the old African Proverb often reminds me, "smooth seas do not make skillful sailors".

Strength is in doing what's right, even if it's painful.

Sekhmet is the guardian/arbiter of Ma'at, which in the Egyptian belief, is the principle of truth. Well, not only truth—it's the natural ordering of the cosmos, that inexorable force that makes everything from the tiniest atoms to the vastest galaxies move along their course. It's that innate sense of justice that makes us balk at wrong doings and great tragedies on personal, community, or global scales. It's the sense of balance that keeps everything just so, and Sekhmet was often known as "The One Who Loves Ma'at and Who Detests Evil".[3] Needless to say, as someone who served Sekhmet, my sense of what's right and wrong and what should be done to uphold the right was greatly developed and put into the spotlight-—and more and more, I began to see that doing the right thing was not always simple. There were times—at work, at school, or in my

---

[3] http://www.ancientegyptonline.co.uk/Sekhmet.html

personal life—that doing the right thing had painful repercussions. Nevertheless, had I not done what was right, it would have hurt my sense of myself as a moral person, and may even have had more negative repercussions on me and on those around me. I am more than sure that many of us can think of times that we've had to make hard decisions, painful decisions, that in the end were the right ones. In my life, it is Sekhmet who helps me be strong enough to make those decisions.

Anger, correctly applied, is a valuable tool.

Sekhmet is famous for her wrathfulness—many are familiar with the myth in which she nearly destroys mankind, who was planning to usurp Ra, and the gods made her drunk in order to calm her bloodlust. In ancient Egypt, there was a statue of Sekhmet for each day of the year, and her priesthood would perform placatory rituals before them to turn aside her great anger.[4]

It shouldn't be a surprise, then, that one of the lessons Sekhmet taught me was one of anger, its power, and how anger is best used. Anger can be the root of many problems—unbalanced anger creates hatred, breaks up communities and friendships, and is at the root of many a war. And yet, righteous anger is also at the root of many great movements which have led to greater freedoms. Examining our own history, especially in our civil rights movements, one can see how anger at injustice leads many to take brave, progressive steps in changing the proverbial lay of the land, making life better for those who came after them. Anger, in itself, is not an evil thing—it is its misuse that creates evil. Just as Sekhmet's wrath nearly destroyed a rebellious humanity, it is also Sekhmet's wrath that protects the pharaoh, that drives out the evils and injustice that offends Ma'at.

---

[4] http://www.egyptiandreams.co.uk/sekhmet.php

Destruction is necessary for new growth.

A very wise friend once told me, "Nobody loves the razor—even as it cuts the cancer from you, it still hurts. And if you are a razor in the paw of Sekhmet, she discards you once you are dulled." I both agreed and disagreed with him, and I'll explain how.

It is true that destruction of any kind can be painful, traumatic, and has the capacity to be completely life-changing. No one likes to see their world turned upside down, no one likes to give up the things they're worked hard to maintain, even if they're stifling illusions that have blocked them from advancing in their life as a spiritual or better person. Yes, the razor which cuts your cancer from you hurts like hell, but it's also a hurt that is healing and purifying—the destruction of your old life and the decay of your illusions provides nourishment for your new life, for new truths to come to light. This process can be seen in the natural life cycles (in which plants grow through the decay of other plants) and in the process of alchemy (*nigredo, albedo, cinitras* and *rubedo*): destruction is necessary for new life. So, while I agree with my friend that no one likes the razor to hurt them, I think that the wise are grateful for the existence of said razor.

Secondly, I would like to address the second part of his statement. I do agree that Sekhmet does not suffer fools lightly, and earlier, I talked about how if you fail to learn your life lessons, you become dulled. However, I can speak from personal experience: Sekhmet does not abandon those that she loves. Sometimes even good cubs get hurt in the wild, and cry out in the wilderness for their mother. You may be dulled, or hurt, or unable to stand on your own—but one who knows Sekhmet as their goddess can know that she is there for them, ready to lend us her strength until we are ready to learn to walk on our own again. And even so, she is with us, guiding our steps.

Meeting Sekhmet
Anne Kreilcamp

Last November, I received another letter from Deidre inviting me to tour Egypt for two weeks with a group of women in late January. The first letter I threw away. I stopped to read the second one, and then was so moved by the idea of this journey that I immediately fired off a reply detailing why I *absolutely could not come.* Too much money.

A few days later, I dreamed that small obstacles were preventing me from going on a trip abroad with some women. What I found interesting about the dream was that when I woke up I was furious! How could I have let those little things stop me! As soon as Jeff woke up, I told him about the dream. A few minutes later, I told him about Deidre's letters and how I had responded to the second one. Oddly enough, I made no conscious connection between the trip to Egypt and the dream! But Jeff did, and said "Well then, we'll have to make sure you can go."

That was it. Right then and there, I resolved to go to Egypt, no matter what it took. I had $1500 in savings, and I could borrow on my credit cards if need be. Then, amazingly enough, my parents and my in-laws volunteered the rest of the money. (This kind of gifting has happened only one other time in my life, so I was certainly not expecting it.)

Why circumstances had miraculously cleared the way for this journey was not clear, though I had always wanted to go, ever since I was a child staring at pictures in art history books, wondering why I felt so connected to the art of ancient Egypt and Greece, why it seemed so eerily familiar. (This was long before I had ever heard of reincarnation; I was a good Catholic girl.)

In 1990, my friend Clarissa and I had saved our money for a year so we could spend a month in Greece uncovering the Goddess in ancient ruins; now, with only six weeks' notice, I would go to Egypt. Little did I know it then, but on my journey to Egypt, I would undergo death and resurrection, paralleling the myth of Osiris.

Day three, at the hotel in Giza, from my journal: *Have been unable to sleep. Last night, asking my inner guides, and the only message I got was 'Open.' Then, when I did, a terrible feeling of oppression on my solar plexus, what I have previously described as 'an infinite hole of negativity'—and it felt like a giant hand had its fist closed around my stomach and was yanking up on it... Towards morning, still sleepless, the feeling that there may be a 'force field' set up around ancient secrets.* The Great Pyramid towered over our hotel, not even a quarter-mile away. I hope that once we left Giza, I would be able to sleep.

The day before, we had visited the "Serapeum," near the step pyramid at Saqqara. The Serapeum is a series of enormous underground vaulted hallways offset with twenty-four niches the size of large bedrooms, each of which contains a huge sarcophagus meant for a bull. Walking through the shadowy hallways of the Serapeum had left me with an eerie feeling, the odd sense that I was contaminated with something from that ancient time.

The next morning, besides feeling exhausted from lack of sleep, I also felt lethargic, drugged. Attempting to shake it off, I continued with the group on our tours of ancient tombs and temples and the grand old Egyptian Museum in Cairo.

On the cruise boat, anchored at Luxor, day four, from journal: *Despite sleep last night, still feel fairly week, sometimes chilled, sometimes feverish. Pain in muscles going up and down stairs.*

Day six, journal: *I've been conserving my energy so that I have enough for the antiquities each morning. I then collapse into bed, and mostly sleep until the next morning's call, at 7:30. So lethargic, I'm almost paralyzed.* I told Hope, my roommate, that I had somehow locked into the shadow of ancient Egypt. That it was as if "my Ka had gone down into the Ba." (From our Egyptian guide, I had learned that the KA is the soul, and that C.G. Jung identified the BA as the collective unconscious.) We both laughed at my strange remark. And we both knew that, somehow, it was true. I was the only one to be having this kind of experience.

Day eight, journal: *Woke up today hoping to feel much better after Deidre volunteered a wonderful Reiki healing on me last night. I told her that I had been feeling awful, leaden, paralyzed. Working mostly on my legs, she was 'told to tell' me 'to accept the quickening.' She was also told to tell me that 'I have an Ankh in my womb.'* (The Ankh is the symbol of everlasting life.)

I told her that it was as if I had come here and contacted the shadow of ancient Egypt, that I was holding it—for everyone—the same way I did with the shadow of Hiroshima as a two-year-old child. She said, "You must birth that now, let it go."

Before Deidre worked on me, I told her that I didn't think I would make it to the temple complex at Karnak the next day. That every day I was feeling a little worse, and had been only barely able to make it to the Dendara temple that morning. She told me that before we went to the main complex at Karnak, if I could get up the energy, to at least go to a small shrine on the outskirts, one dedicated to the goddess Sekhmet. She said that she had had a powerful experience when she first went there, and she thought that I would too, since lion-headed Sekhmet was known as the dark side of the Hathor (Aphrodite) energy. That Sekhmet held the shadow. One of her most-told stories goes like this: when the god Ra was getting old, he started to lose the respect of his people. So he asked Hathor to do something to make them regain their respect. Hathor came to Ra in her aspect as Sekhmet, and her solution to the problem was to go on a killing rampage, becoming so bloodthirsty that not even the gods could stop her. Finally Ra had to trick her to stop, by making up a sleeping potion for her to drink which looked like blood.

So the next morning, once again, I forced myself to get up and dress and eat a little breakfast, and follow the group from our cruise boat to our little bus. I wasn't feeling better, which was discouraging; on the other hand, I wasn't feeling worse either. So maybe Deidre's work had shifted the energy, halted the descent.

Strangely enough, when we approached the little shrine, I was first in line (usually I dragged behind). The outside doorway led into the central one of three rooms, which contained the statue of a headless seated god. Before I had a chance to investigate this statue, I felt like I was being pulled to the right, to enter a darkened room. Peeking around the corner (why was I peeking? did I already know that I would be afraid?) I was instantly galvanized by what looked like two eyes, gleaming in the darkness. Looking right at me, they were fierce, alien, even extraterrestrial. Hope, who had been right behind me, heard me whisper, "Oh my God!" — as if I was terrified. I *was* terrified. I felt like a small child who had just seen the bogeyman.

I was not the only one to experience the statue of Sekhmet in this manner. Even the skeptical, intellectual Britisher in our group came up to me afterwards to say, in a surprised, hushed voice, "She was *terrifying!*"

Deidre had arranged for our Egyptian guide to take the guards away from the little shrine so we could have the place to ourselves for awhile. Each woman then spent a few minutes alone in the room with the Sekhmet statue. When I went in there, I was surprised to see that the room had gotten lighter, and that I had mistakenly taken her ears to be her eyes! (At the time, I took this to be a stupid mistake on my part; after the trip was over, I came across an author, Robert Masters, who thinks that ancient Egyptian statues were sometimes deliberately constructed to give two distinctly different impressions.) I could see now that her real eyes were not frightening, but utterly compassionate. However, the energy in the statue as a whole, or maybe it was just in that part of the little room she was in (unlike many statues, this was still standing in the place it had originally occupied), was extraordinarily uncanny and powerful. When my turn came, I entered Her presence feeling embarrassed and abashed, like a serf facing a queen. Standing about five feet in front of her, I closed my eyes and my head instantly filled with what I can only describe as a continuous loud deep buzzing. The energy was so overwhelming that I opened my eyes, and again, the unbearable, inaudible, screaming buzz—I closed my eyes again. Still the energy sounded in me—overwhelming. I opened my eyes. There was no escape from it. I surrendered, moving into resonance with the powerful uncanny energy in that room.

Several of us remarked, after re-emerging from our own audiences with Sekhmet, that the room she was in was becoming lighter, and, since the sky was clear and the room constructed of stone, we wondered how that was happening. When our sessions were over, we went to find our guide, as he wanted to say a few things to us about Sekhmet. *Five minutes later, when he walked into the room, it had returned to its original darkness.* Again, several of us noted this.

That afternoon I felt marginally better, and told Deidre that perhaps her session with me had helped after all, because I wasn't worse that day, that perhaps Reiki had helped to turn the tide. The next morning I awoke spontaneously at 5:30 and was moved to go out and watch the sunrise. As I sat on the deck watching the sun rise over the Nile, I realized that I felt better, much better; that this new day was a new birth. That same morning I learned that besides being the dark goddess, resembling Kali, Sekhmet was also the goddess of disease and healing!

That afternoon, I suddenly realized that my meeting with Sekhmet was the reason I had come to Egypt. That, as I had been paralyzed by the collective nuclear shadow in this life since I was a small child, so I had also, on going to Egypt, assumed the weight of the collective shadow of this ancient land. Indeed, if reincarnation is to be a factor here, perhaps it was in Egypt when I first picked up this energy, as if it was my own to carry, and that in coming back to Earth in 1942, only three weeks after the first Chicago experiment in nuclear fission, I was, because of my ancient Egyptian experience, primed to take on collective shadow energy again in this life. In coming into the presence of the power of Sekhmet, in moving into resonance with her terrible and compassionate energy, I had given that shadow back to the god, where it belonged. Only She could contain the collective shadow energy. I was a mere mortal; I had no business carrying such a horrendous weight.

Soon after arriving home, I sent my trip journal to one of my sisters. Imagine my shock when she responded via email: *Not long after JP (a famous European opera producer, and her lover for many years) died, he appeared in a dream and said 'The KA is the BA.'* I didn't know what that meant at the time and ran to the New York Public Library to find out.

Messages From Sekhmet

Ana Anpuhemet

Written by Ana Anpuhemet on 11/27/05 upon return home from a pilgrimage to the Temple of Goddess Spirituality Dedicated to Sekhmet located in Indian Springs, NV.

As I take my journal out of my bag for the first serious time since returning home a week ago, I am reminded of the lovely smell of the Temple. The pages are touched with the scent of the daily sacrificial fires from the temple. It had become a nightly ritual for me that sometimes even started at 1 or 2pm. I would gather my humble offerings of incense and beads together, bring some nuts and seeds for food offerings and for myself. I brought my song folder to sing and my riq to accompany me. And then my journal...

My journal was a constant staple, a security blanket of sorts. As long as I had that to record, somehow it made the craziness more real. The things I witnessed and were put through were not as crazy and farfetched as I was sure they would appear to others. It was my proof that I really did do this journey, what They had asked of me. My proof that I kept my word and They, Theirs. My proof that I passed to the next level. My proof and reminder of how blessed I am.

This is an excerpt from my journal I would like to share. This is the night I was given several new names, or I should say, old and forgotten names, of Sekhmet. Part of the daily homage that people perform is chanting the 108 known names of Sekhmet. According to Robert Masters in his book The Goddess Sekhmet, *there are 4000 names of Sekhmet in total, 2000 of which are known only to the Gods, another 1000 known only to the priests, and the last 1000 were known to common man. Only 108 survive now. Part of the project for the temple is collecting more of Her names to recite in Her honor. Sekhmet blessed me with a few more of Her names in this entry and my first full day there. We got down to business really quickly.*

November 9th, Wednesday:

After the temple priestess left the temple, I stayed and continued the fire. It will be a long night. Even leaving for just a moment to get food and my journal made Her unhappy; the fires roared and spit sparks. I assured Her I'd be back and they subsided. I gave Her a clove cigarette and we smoked together. She gave me a few more of Her names; Lady of the Flaming Mane, Lady of the Silent Roar Within, and Lady of the Path.

She had me set Anpu's statue on the pedestal at Her feet. She originally wanted Him on Her lap so that He would have maximum recognition, but I thought it better to have Him less conspicuous. She requested I place Him in the temple to honor that He was present, and that His wife had come to Her as agreed. She explained that it was an honor to have us visit Her. Funny, I thought I was the one who should feel so honored, and I do. She is so gracious and formidable, I don't feel I deserve the courtesy and pomp and circumstance She's shown me. She wants me at Her feet (sitting at the foot of Her statue), even though I am reluctant to block the fire from Her. It is so warm and inviting.

Lady of the Sacred Flame. I've always found Sekhmet to be a lot like Brighid in Her many aspects. I am honored that the Gods talk to me at all. I know They are different Goddesses, but having worked with both, I see Their similarities and individuality though They share a common name.

Finder of the Ways, Revealer of the Ancient Paths, Keeper of Those She Holds Dear, Heart's Flame, Lady of the Purifying Fire, Inspiration of Humankind, Wrath of Ra, She Who is the Flame Within the Darkness, Keeper of the Light, She Who is the Precious Flame of Hope.

I am being sent to bed early so I can be worked on in my sleep. It's only 10pm, but feels much later to my East Coast body. I left Her with some Nag Champa even though She wanted Frankincense. She was fine with that, but I will need to bring it in the morning.

November 13th, Sunday:

As I sat around the fire and caught up on my journaling, a spider crawled on me. I didn't go in to a panic (I was a severe arachnophobic up until 2 months ago), but I did flick him off. Then I felt bad because I hadn't realized I aimed towards the fire, so I apologized and hoped I hadn't killed it, and I began looking for it. When I gave up a few minutes later, after Sekhmet kept telling me I hadn't hurt it, it crawled on me again—I guess to tell me it was fine or maybe wanted to be friends. I don't know, but I'm not ready for that level of interaction. This time I aimed it away from the fire and flicked it off again. I think it was trying to tell me that we have business, and we do, which I am dreading. Though I don't freak as I used to, I'm still not fond of them.

The scorpion found in the temple over the summer was right by Selket's statue, I am told; how appropriate. I've been giving Her incense and candles for the help She gave me two months ago, which incidentally cured me of my severe arachnophobia. I decided that, instead of doing my spider meditation, I will ask Sekhmet what message She would like to have relayed to Her followers.

Her response was; "I came to this desert many years ago as a guardian and protectress. I watched humanity rise with all its wonders, but I also saw its fall in the ease it brought. You became dependent on so much and forgot the ways we did things and why. Each task has its purpose. Each deed has its offering. Each offering is sacred, and you as humans have lost that to a great extent. Sacredness comes in what you do to connect yourself to others. A smile is sacred, letting someone know you are happy to see them, helping others. Helping yourself (pause) is sacred.

"All too often, you forget to view yourselves as sacred. The Gods and Goddesses exist within you. Treat yourselves as a temple. Recognize the sacredness you give to others. See how this connects you to the universe as a whole. Recognize your place within this whole. Remember that always. I stand watch over that which humanity has burdened us with. I sit ready to rise and abolish the evil that threatens. I am the Mother of the Caring Heart, but I am also She Who Perseveres in Times of Struggle. I am not afraid to take this burden of *guardian* and in this place, that is what I am.

"But to guard humans from themselves can only come so far. I need your help, your commitment. Sit ready to lead the fight against the burden some still fuel. But more important, let this change begin with you by remembering the sacredness and passing it along to others. Perhaps then I will not need to be as on guard on land so abused by the burdens humanity bestows."

I am totally exhausted after that. That channel took a lot out of me, oddly enough. I curled up by the fire after nearly nodding off on the pillows by the Virgine de Guadalupe (She has a shrine there). I slept for about 45 minutes, maybe more. I tried getting my head together but I'm too cold, and that Sekhmet talk took a lot out of me. It was almost like She took over my writing, or at least was dictating so fast I could barely keep up.

I am released to be able to go to bed now, and I am being allowed to sleep in the guest house with heat. I did my good-nights and left.

Sekhmet
Marcus

She has been prominent in my life, and I owe her a great debt as well. I felt her in Kuwait in 2003. It was my first deployment, and I felt so lost. My leadership was not always understanding of my feelings, beliefs, or concerns. However, Sekhmet came to me and comforted me.

I cannot honor her enough. She is a Goddess of great power and intensity. At the same time, she can be so comforting. Her rage is one inspired by the violation of Ma'at. Through her, I have learned to be a warrior. I learned to toughen up. Now she reminds me that some things are worth fighting for. Some things are worth dying for. Freedom isn't free. Everything has a price. In my opinion, she teaches the lessons of Fehu and Gebo (the Norse runes of Value and Gifting) quite nicely. Sacrifice is part of life. Right action is not a request. It is a requirement. Sekhmet also reminds me that being a warrior is not a part-time job, but a way of life.

Prayers and Invocations

Daily Prayer
Galina Krasskova

Lady of Power,
I commend myself into Your hands.
Open me, burn me, purify
until in my heart
there is only You.

Sekhmet
Rebecca Buchanan

She is the scarlet one
the mistress of dread
the lady of slaughter
who wields the seven arrows:
earthquake
flood
drought
pestilence
famine
war
healing

brilliant
blinding
scorching as midday
is Sekhmet

Hymn to Sekhmet

Galina Krasskova

Before I ever knew Your name,
I knew Your touch.
In the soulless wasteland of my childhood
You were my strength.
From the darkest anguish of my heart,
Your light guided me forward.
You succored me when it seemed no one else cared.
You tempered me when it seemed I would fail
in the simplest of devotions.
Beloved Mother, in the bitterest hour of my need,
I tasted Your fire. I drank of its strength.
I was blessed with Your love and Your protection.
Your fire, Sekhmet, is my joy.
Your embrace is my comfort,
and my homecoming.
Oh, Mother Sekhmet,
anneal the clay of Your warrior's heart.
Keep me, Goddess, from all complaisance.
Burn me free of all hubris, Lady of courage and strength.
Fierce Goddess, teach me the law of Your fire,
that I might know You in strength as well as in sorrow.
I would bring You joy as well as tears,
laughter as well as the fervor of my battle-hungry heart.
Nourisher of my Heart, Lady of the House of Life
You who are the Force against which no other force may stand,
May I ever find favor in Your sight.
Homage to You, Beloved Sekhmet.

This was written over ten years ago, after I had first been taken in hand by
Sekhmet. It was first published in *Heart of the Sun: An Anthology in
Exaltation of Sekhmet* by Candace Kant and Anne Key, Goddess Ink, 2011.

A Prayer To Sekhmet

Marcus

Ancient Goddess and Protectress, I call to you.
Eye of Ra and Righter of Wrongs, I honor you.
Mother and Teacher of Warriors, I embrace you.

I kneel before you without any secrets.
You know my strengths and weaknesses.
With your instruction, I know righteousness.

I humbly request that you allow me to be of service.
Please allow me to embrace all of you with great reverence.
Thank you for your lessons and generous benevolence.

Blessed Protector of Ra and Maat, I give you my devotion.
You are worthy of glory, praise, and meditation.
Thank you for helping set my warrior path in motion.

Great Goddess of Healing, I am humbled and revived by your touch.
You have changed my life forever and given me so much.
Please allow me to bring honor to you instead of using you as a
crutch.

Lady and Lioness of the Sun, I uplift you.
Sekhmet, Powerful One, I keep you in my heart so true.
You are mighty beyond comprehension, and I give you your due!

Prayer of Protection
Kira R.

Sekhmet, Mother of Power
Protect me for I am Your child.
Gird me against the
Plots of my enemies.
Wrap me in the protective wall
Of Your flame,
Strike them down.
Oh Goddess,
Against Whom no opponent
May stand,
I call to You in my need.
Warrior,
Vaniquisher.
Now and always,
I praise Thee.

Daughter of Sekhmet

Stephania Ebony

Robe of scarlet silk,
skin scented with cinnabar,
necklace of red jasper and sardonyx,
dark auburn mane plaited
with fine filaments of crimson and gold.
No one doubts to Whom you belong.

The Temple dancers ask you
if the Nile is red with blood or beer.
You read the thirst in their eyes
and interpret the position of the sun overhead
with respect to the point of the largest pyramid.

The span is short from season to season,
ritual to pageant to festival to celebration.
The Nile floods, then subsides.
The cruel sun reveals thin parchment skin
stretched taut across your cheekbones.

Have the dead been tended yet today?
Wrapped in sacred linen,
permeated with macerated herbs?
Is the gilded paint dry yet
on your sarcophagus?

"A grand occasion," the temple sages say.
The closing of one eye of Ra
means the opening of another.
Who will remember you
but the One you serve?

After your stilled heart is weighed

and measured against a feather,
your spirit will rise to reign with your Mother,
your name lost in history.

Fierce Sekhmet
Amanda Sioux Blake

Hail Sekhmet, mighty lioness!
Fierce warrior, most powerful
Your anger burns hot
Burns as the rays of the sun
For You are the Hand of Horus,
The feminine face of the sun
Consort of Ptah, You fiery spark
That brings manifestation
But also destruction
So staunch a guardian of right order
You are so enraged by injustice
That You may slip into the blood-red haze of violence
That wise Thoth once pulled You out of
Great Lioness of the Desert
Fierce Sekhmet, I will remember You.

Five Invocations of Sekhmet

Ana Anpuhemet

Artist Invocation

Sekhmet! Lady of the Arts!
Inspiration of Humankind
She Whose Opportunity Escapeth Her Not
At Whose Wish the Arts Were Born
Beautiful Face, Image Most Beloved By Art
Inspirer of Males
Sparkling One
The Source
Lady of Enchantments
You who inspire beauty and grace
You who craft life and forge anew,
May you inspire the Artist within
That we may make our lives
Into the work of art set forth by the Divine.

Destructor Invocation

Sekhmet! Lady of Destruction!
Lady of the Bloodbath
Destroyer by Plagues
Destroyer of Rebellions
Wander in the Wastes
Destroyer by Fire
Devouring One
Burner of Evildoers
Terrible One
Wrath of Ra
One Before Whom Evil Trembles
You who has the courage to face that which no longer should be
You who are unafraid to demolish those
Who would betray and act dishonorably
May you awaken the Destructor within
That we may cleanse true injustices from ourselves and our lives.

Healer Invocation

Sekhmet! Lady of Healing!

Pure One

Complete One

Lady of the Waters of Life

Lady of the Way of the Five Bodies

Goddess of Love

Great Lady of the House of Life

Lady of the Purifying Flame

Reminder of the Sweetness of Life

You who cleanse us of our ills

You who makes whole that which is incomplete

May you fill the Healer within

That we find the courage to fix which has been broken

Warrior/Protectress Invocation

Sekhmet! Lady Warrior and Protectress!

Protectress of the Gods

Victorious One in Battles

Overcomer of All Enemies

Guide and Protectress from the Perils of the Underworld

Unrivaled and Invincible One

Warrior Goddess

Protectress of the Divine Order

Protectress of the Ancient Ways

Keeper of the Light

You who is the defender of the weak

You who are the spirit of the strong

May you ignite the Warrior and Protector within

That we may defend and stand up for our truth.

Teacher Invocation
Sekhmet! Lady of Learning and Great Teacher!
Awakener
Opener of Ways
Lady of Transformations
Enlightener
Empowerer
Great One of Hekau
The Aware
Lady of the House of Books
Beloved Teacher
Lady of the Path
Revealer of Ancient Paths
You who shapes our minds and our lives
You who reveals crucial knowledge of the Divine
May you call forth the Teacher within
That we may find our true path to Sacredness.

The Fiery Lioness
Amanda Sioux Blake

I sing now of the fiery lioness
Fearsome stalker of the desert
Lady of the Sun
Who wipes out evildoers
With Her cleansing rage
Winged Ra's avenger, hot justice unleashed
With Wadjet, venom-spitting cobra, You purify the world
Panting fury, hands bloodied red
Heated breath burning away impurity

I pray You, Fierce Sekhmet
Heed Thoth's soothing words
Cease to be the Devouring One
Cease to be the Ruler of Serpents and of Dragons
Cease to be the Wanderer of the Wastes
Cease to be the Lady of the Bloodbath
Cease to be the Destroyer By Fire
Cease to be the Terrible One
Cease to be the Roamer of Deserts
Cease to be the Flaming One
Cease to be the Destroyer of Rebellions
Cease to be the She Who is Divine Vengeance

I was torn on the inclusion of this piece. I find it beautifully written, but I would not wish for Sekhmet to be other than what She is: a fierce Warrior, Bringer of destruction. I deplore the tendency in some Neo-Pagan circles to attempt to soften Her. That, however, is not what is going on here, and the text is in line with traditional prayers to Sekhmet. Since it was offered in respect, I chose to include it here despite my ambivalence. – GK

I pray You, Gentle Sekhmet
Heed Thoth's soothing words
Become once more the Self-Contained
Become once more the Beautiful Light
Become once more the Great One of Healing
Become once more the Beloved Teacher
Become once more the Pure One
Become once more the Giver of Ecstasies
Become once more the Bountiful One
Become once more the Lady of Enchantments
Become once more the Satisfier of Desires
Become once more the Lady of the Waters of Life

Follow the Scribe docilely to Your home in Memphis
Join again with Your husband Ptah, Lord of Life
He Who knows the name of everything
For all things issue forth from Him
Together there is balance
Death with Life
Destruction with creation
Fire with green plants
Neither overtaking the other
As it should be.

Hail the Fiery Lioness,
Fierce Sekhmet!
And Hail also to Her Husband,
Blue-faced Ptah, Maker of all things!
Hail to the Two Gods of Memphis!

Hymn to Sekhmet II
Rebecca Buchanan

Glory!
Glory! I sing
To the Fierce One
Sekhmet
Alluring Wife of the Craftsman
Tender Mother of the Lotus-Crowned
Furious Daughter of the Sun
Sekhmet
To the Great-Mawed Lioness
Glory! I sing
Glory!

Prayer to Sekhmet
Rebecca Buchanan

Lioness
Wrathful Daughter of the Sun
Father enthroned upon Your head
Heart of divine fire
Who consumes the enemies of the Gods
          in blood and flame
Who consumes the diseases of mind and body
          in blood and flame:

Protect me with Your fire.

Sekhmet: Mother and Protectress

Marcus

Eye of Ra, upholder of Maat, I honor you.
Your warmth heals my heavy heart.
It is by your inspiration that I hold true.
Your courage penetrates me and takes hold of every part.
Your motivation sends me on a journey overdue.

You came to me when I was at war.
By your hand, I came back safely.
I owe you a debt that extends so far.
Your lessons came so passionately.
Without pause, you became my star.

You are the protector of Ra and Maat.
I cannot honor you enough.
Mother and teacher of warriors, you are that
And so much more as you remind me to be tough.
The world can be very rough and as annoying as a gnat.

Great Goddess, blessed Lioness of the Sun,
You are mighty beyond imagination!
Your name means *Powerful One*, and I run
To you to praise and glorify you without hesitation.
You teach me both the art of war and how to have fun.

Patron of physicians, Goddess of Healing, I adore you!
By your awesome power, I am healed and transformed.
Your presence in my life has yielded many rewards undue.
You are generous beyond comprehension, and I am deeply moved.
May my life be pleasing to the one
Who has held me together like glue.

Ancient One of enormous power and wisdom,

You have shaped my anger
Into a blade that I might be a warrior in a world so full of hatred.
Intolerance takes up residence
In the hearts of humankind and danger
Exists in many places foreign and domestic as morals are abated.
Right action emanates from you,
And your willingness to help a stranger.

I came to you from a different path, a different belief.
Yet, you cared for me and tended my wounds so tenderly.
You provide me with nourishment and much needed relief.
Your energy is kind, loving, and full of intensity.
In your presence, all of my worries and concerns are so brief.

Glory be to you, Sekhmet! You are greatly loved
May you always be honored and praised!

Trembling Before Her
Kira R.

She is called Mother of the Dead,
and I lay myself down before Her.

I press my brow against the feet of Her image,
whispering in my heart this prayer:

Oh Great Lady
Whose light cleanses all dark places,
Whose power rises up from the earth,
searing and hot like the desert wind,

Whose anger is a thing
even the other Gods fear,

Who knows the passages
all the dead must traverse
and Who guards those corridors well:

Bring my dead to a place of peace.
Bring my dead to a place of power.
Bring my dead to the place of their soul,
and may their hearts be light on the scales of Anubis.

Your benediction be upon them,
Warrior and Keeper,
of all who walk the paths of darkness
with courage seeking Your light.

Your benediction be upon them
and upon all those who give their dead
honor, respect, and remembrance.

Eldest of All
Great Lady,
Whose light cleanses all dark places,
May the blessing of Your light and fire cleanse me too.

Honor to Sekhmet.
Honor and Praise to the Mother of Power.

A Song For Sekhmet

Serena Toxicat

I was shattered
Like Osiris
Spoke Her name to
Emerging light
I'd been holding
shards together
Somehow

Sekhmet Mender
Of Ma'at
Healed my distress
Unified my parts

I was fractured
Like the sunshine
Held Her image
In my mind
I'd been sending
Splinters out to
Fetch light

Sekhmet Mother
Healed my fragments
Birthed my wholeness
In quiet night

Sekhmet As Healer

Ilyssa Silfen

O harsh Mother
Eater of Blood
Lady of Flame
Eyes black as coal, churning and restless as fire,
Flowing mane cascading down Your shoulders,
Seething mouth opened wide,
A ferocious roar escaping from between Your blood soaked teeth,
Searing breath burning my skin.
You reach into my chest with Your savage claws
And pull out my heart.
"It needs to be burned," You explain.
The bitter tears flow freely from You and from me
As my tender heart crackles in Your purifying fires
And is reduced to ashes.
I reach one hand forward to collect what is left,
But You bat it away with Yours.
I ask You pleadingly with my eyes, "Why?"
You reply with Yours, "Wait."
You place Your hands over the ashes,
Nails caked with dried blood,
And growl menacingly at them, demanding rebirth.
I feel Your sweltering heat coaxing new life forth from death
And I watch as from the ashes my heart grows anew
And once again my heart is on fire.

Appropriate Action

Melia Suez

Lady Sekhmet, Protective Lioness
hear my plea.
Guide me to appropriate actions
when dealing with my son,
my family and friends,
acquaintances and strangers,
and last but not least, myself.
Help me to quench my destructive anger
when it will do more harm than good.
Help me to be passionate when necessary
and staid or quiet when it is not.
Help me to know when to be helpful
and when to leave things alone.
As Lady of Appropriate Action
I ask for your help and guidance.
Honor is yours oh, Mighty Eye of Ra.

Eye of Re

P. Sufenas Virius Lupus

I sing of the Eye of Re –
but not the fiery eye of destruction,
that brought Rome low at Arausio
and Egypt at Actium –
the purifying Eye of Re,
warm breath across space,
unutterable eternal silence
spanning aeons and stadia
separating source from end,
the flaming glow of orange
across and along horizons
that renews each day's strength
and is the compassionate roar
of lioness averting danger,
protective of her children
in the dusk that relieves
the severity of noon and summer,
the Eye of Re quenched
in the sacred lake daily.
Sekhmet the indomitable I sing,
for no mother rages harshly
to desiccate her lotus offspring
without end, without ceasing.
Sunlight falls on all equally,
heating the just, burning the wicked,
each to flower or fall
as she clearly sees fit.

The Lions of Egypt
P. Sufenas Virius Lupus

Antinous emerged from the shallow pool,
his papyrus boat nowhere to be seen.
All was darkness, but before him he saw seated
a lion-headed, bare-breasted goddess.

There were other figures in the shadows,
indistinct, their onyx-black eyes glinting
in the light spilling from above,
a winged eye of lapis lazuli wreathed in flame.

"Lucius Antinous of Bithynion-Claudiopolis,
son of Mantinoë and Hermogenes, of Arcadian blood,
kin to sun and moon, bear-mother and wolf-sire,
you stand before this tribunal with blood on your hands."

What was happening? Had he not been rowing,
had a falcon not flown over his head
and he glanced toward it in the noonday sun,
dazzled and blinded, then falling, flailing...

"You are accused of having a hand in the death
of a lion, the very image of the sun triumphant.
He who would strike at the sun itself
commits a gross act of sacrilege, of hubris."

"I state in my defense only these two things:
first, for my offense the lion nearly killed me,
and if I did not respect the beast before,
then surely beneath its wrath I was in deepest awe."

The shapes in shadow stirred, not silent,
a multitude of whispers and murmuring,
while in a circuit the circle of flames sped up,
changing from red-orange to blue-green around the eye.

"Second, I note the circumstance of this attack:
I was in the company of the Sovereign of the Two Lands,
who was ridding the land of a ravenous scourge -
he who is the image of the Sun on earth struck himself."

The flames circled faster, to white, to black,
a sound like the whining of metal against metal
as the shapes in darkness muttered more loudly.
"Do you then deny your guilt before this tribunal?"

"No, I only seek to give an account of my actions."
The tumult among the shadows became deafening,
then the lion-goddess struck her sceptre three times
against the stone floor of the tribunal chamber.

"Antinous, you have contributed to the loss
of a star from a constellation during the holy month
when the lion is preeminent among the stars,
when the heavens become the likeness of a lion.

"Therefore, your sentence is clear to this court:
it is your work of aeons eternal to replace this loss,
to become a new lion where the old once was,
to restore the cosmos where chaos crept in."

The eye above shimmered and closed,
and materializing behind it stood a giant,
lion-headed, encoiled and bound in a serpent,
neither wholly male nor female, winged, roaring.

"The lions of Egypt have made their decree –
you are to be counted among our number,
a protector and liberator in times of distress,
a balm and succor to the defenseless in their need."

From the shadows emerged two figures:
a young man in a blue headdress, lotus-crowned,
and a ram-headed man crowned with three cobras,
each in turn adorned with a solar disc.

"I, Sekhmet, shall be your mother;
Nefertem-Maahes shall be your brother;
and your father shall be he who is above strength,
he upon the banks and the lake, Heryshaf.

"Upon the shores of Djehuty's holy city,
may the scribe-god record it well:
the red lotus flower will be named for Antinous,
the memorial of the death of the lion."

The waters in the pool stirred, burst their sides,
and the wrath of the Eye of Re was averted,
the inundation returned to the Two Lands,
and Antinous' star appeared in the heavens.

*(Pachrates the Egyptian of Heliopolis, learned in the mysteries, wrote this
in honor of the Re-Osiris of Herakleopolis and of the Osiris of Antinoöpolis.)*

A Prayer To Sekhmet

Galina Krasskova

Mother, burn me.
Let me dance in Your searing flames.
Warrior, pierce me,
Tear away the masks,
Tear away the burdens of my ego.
Free my spirit.
Devour me.
Mold me in Your burning hands,
Mother of courage, Mother of terror.
Embrace me, that in dying in Your scorching flames,
I might live.
Mother, give me burning.

Awakening of Sekhmet

Ana Anpuhemet

Awaken great Lady of the Sun,
Come to us at our invitation,
Burn brightly in our hearts and minds
Breathe your purifying breath in to us
Make right what has been wronged
Make strong what has grown weak
Make true which has become false
Restore what has been lost
Awaken great Lady of the Sun
Rise and walk with us
Our hearts call you
Awaken and rise!

Awakening of Sekhmet with Egyptian Translation

Ana Anpuhemet

(The first line is Ancient Egyptian, the second is the English translation.)

Nehes weret nebet Ra
Awaken Great Lady of the Sun

Iu-ne ne iauss
Come to us at our invitation
(Awaken and arise)

Het weben-te ab-ne hen' tep-ne
Burn brightly in our hearts
(Awaken and arise)

Teper-te we'eb nefet neb
Breathe your purifying breath into us
(Awaken and arise)

Ir Ma'at wenet wenen nef
Make right what has been wronged
(Awaken and arise)

Ir nehet r'ed bedes
Make strong what has grown weak
(Awaken and arise)

Ir we'eb neb gereg
Make true that which has become false
(Awaken and arise)

Di sa' wenet wenen nen gem
Restore what has been lost
(Awaken and arise)

Nehes weret nebet Ra
Awaken Great Lady of the Sun

He'ei 'h'-ne
Rise and walk with us
(Awaken and arise)

Hety-ne iauss-ek
Our hearts call to you

Nehes hen' he'ei!
Awaken and arise!

Sekhmet

Melitta Benu

Warrior woman, Face of the Sun,
Whose hot breath caresses me like the burning desert winds:
Place the rod and scepter in my hands,
Make my heart hard and crimson as carnelian
So that I might know the meaning of power.
So that I might know the meaning of strength.
That I might know both are rooted in
The beating of your courageous heart.

You, Sekhem Ma'at,
Who runs through my veins like strong wine,
Who makes me drunk from the smell of your skin:
Make me as you are–
Iron wrapped in silk and velvet,
The fiery taste of hot blood and desire,
The feel of sore muscles, dancing
Tapping out the rhythms of life with graceful steps.

Woman of the Blood Soaked Garment,
Razor which strips me,
Knives that flay the cancers from my spirit:
Set the bones of my life
So that they align as towers–
Strong against any onslaught,
Mighty and alive like the Sun over Heliopolis,
And bent in reverence and adoration

To you.
Sekhmet, Great One of Heka.
Sekhmet, Awakener.
Sekhmet, before whom Evil trembles.

An Offering
Setep

Your name is Sweetness, oh my Goddess,
My Goad and my Delight.
You have enveloped me in Your flame.
I am as spice in Your fire.
I anoint myself with Your presence
As with sweetest perfume.
Devouring One, Your bite is bliss.
Tear my soul asunder.
I am Yours – let my existence feed
The bright heat of Your flame,
Oh my Miracle.
Since I was a child,
You have been my promise.
I have followed my Fate to You, my Joy.
You are the Delight of my Manhood,
The Terror of my Days,
My most longed for Feral Sweetness,
Never shall I escape Your power.
Mistress of all that I shall ever be,
Command me.

I seek breath
Only that I might chant the sweet litany of Your sacred names.
I seek body,
Only that I might work Your will
Through hand and heart and action.
I seek agency,
Only that I might restore Your worship to the world, oh Goddess.
Strength of my line, of my bones and my blood,
Marrow of my spirit.
I seek strength only that I might serve You well, in all things.
I am Your slave, Oh Sekhmet.

Sekhmet Call And Response

Ana Anpuhemet

("Hy" means "Hail" hail in Ancient Egyptian)

Beloved Sekhmet, daughter of Ra, hear us...
    Hy Sekhmet!
You who shine in the darkness of our souls...
    Hy Sekhmet!
You who give gifts of healing and knowledge...
    Hy Sekhmet!
You who teach us the way of the ancients...
    Hy Sekhmet!
You who lead us through the dark to our dawn...
    Hy Sekhmet!
You who shine upon us each day...
    Hy Sekhmet!
And curl us in your protective embrace each night...
    Hy Sekhmet!
You who have breathed your purifying breath in to us...
    Hy Sekhmet!
You who burn the falsehoods away and leave the truth...
    Hy Sekhmet!
You who destroy our delusions and open our eyes...
    Hy Sekhmet!
You who give us the strength to become who we are...
    Hy Sekhmet!
You who are deserving of our devotion and praise...
    Hy Sekhmet!
You whom we hail, Hy Sekhmet!

Into Her Abode

Galina Krasskova

A very long time ago,
before I had found my name,
I went to Her sacred place.
I asked for a gift, thinking with envy
on the delicate beauty of those who had guided me,
and I promised service in return.
She looked at me. Into me.
I did not draw back from Her heat
(though it burned me to my core).
"Courage" She said, tossing it to me,
touching me within, where the seed would unfold,
a scarlet tinged, thousand petaled lotus.
It was sharp and it cut deeply.
I thought it paltry gift at the time,
in the face of beauty I had been denied.
Then I saw the things that scurried from the light
and hid in the damp, dark, bleak,
angry places of my soul...
then I saw the gifts to which this first was the key.
I saw and began to understand what a great gift I had been given.
Courage. The warrior's gift.
The only sword capable of bearing me through such darkness.
Then I learned my name.

Sonnet For Sekhmet

Kiya Nicoll

O Lady of the piercing, burning gaze
Flame-wreathed, flame-warded, desert lioness
Whose fearsome vengeance stalks the heart transgressed
Against the law; Whose brilliant shining rays
Allow no flaw to go unmarked. Ablaze,
Her cauterising touch is a caress,
A transformation shaping a distress
Into a strength within Her hands upraised.
How fierce Her countenance, how sure Her will,
How deep Her hunger and how broad Her reach,
How powerful Her voice, how sweet Her breath,
How bottomless Her knowledge and Her skill,
How relentless the discipline She'll teach.
All praise, Sekhmet, who holds both life and death.

Prayer
Galina Krasskova

Beloved Sekhmet,
You bestowed upon me the crown of priestess.
You steeped my hands in ritual
and made devotion my art.
I look back humbled, Mother.
I look back awed by Your kindness
to one who knew so little,
and who brought only an undisciplined spirit
to Your altar.

When first You set my feet upon this path,
that would lead so unerringly to Woden,
I knew only that I wished to serve.
I did not know how or what it might entail,
or the changes that would, of necessity,
be wrought within my heart.
I only knew that I hungered for Your fire,
to be of use in whatever small way You found fitting.
I remember those rituals, the first fearful fumblings
on the road of endless mysteries.
I look back into battered journals,
scribbled notes redolent with zeal
and I see ritual after ritual crafted around *things*:
the athame, fire, chakras and more.
How odd to see a time when I diligently copied
other people's words because I had not yet learned
how to form my own.
I have to laugh now having come, it seems,
so many achingly endless steps from that place...
or maybe not so far.
Things seem so meaningless now.
How funny to make of them the centerpoint of a ritual.

I knew no better at the time but I learned,
stubborn as I was, I learned.

I know one thing, and for this alone
I bow my head and kiss the dirt in gratitude:
It was Your wisdom that taught me how to pray,
and that rituals were meant not for things but for devotion,
for those thoughts and prayers and songs and acts
that make the heart a fertile field for the Gods.
I learned if nothing else, that single lesson well:
to center every ritual, every action,
every day and year and minute around the Gods.
I never realized what a precious gift it was,
this awareness, this yoke of intense focus
with which You bound me.
Only now, a lifetime later, when I have died
and been birthed again from fire and ash and pain,
do I see what a prize I was given so undeservedly.
And though my words are weak,
my heart—because of You—is not:
Thank you, Sekhmet.
My Mother.

Sacredness: A Song For Sekhmet

Ana Anpuhemet

Sun bears down across the desert
Barren land few fruits to give
Aware and alive amidst it all

I walk among you
I live within you
I call forth your sacredness

Crowned and throned I guard and guide you
Offerings left and fires lit
Silent prayers your hearts call to me

I have heard you
I will answer you
I call forth your sacredness

And on this edge of man's own burden
Troubled land that feels it all
Bring forth a change to shift the balance

I call to you
Stand beside me
I call forth your sacredness

I call to you
Stand beside me
I call forth your sacredness.

Sacredness

Ana Anpuhemet

Sun bears down a - cross the des - ert, __ Bar - ren land, few fruits to give. A - ware and a - live a - midst it all, __ I walk a - mong you, I live with - in __ you, I call forth your sa - cred __ ness. __

Rituals and
Meditations

Daily Sekhmet Meditation

Galina Krasskova

This is a very brief elemental rite that can be used daily to honor Sekhmet.

Sekhmet!

Say Her name several times, savor the sounds, savor the intensity, savor its power and resonance. She is the embodiment of power and strength, Her name its mighty hekau.

I stand before You, Mother, ready to receive Your wisdom.
I stand before You, Mother, ready to receive Your strength.
Enfold me in Your fire.
Purify me in Your radiant heat.
Make of me a pristine blade in Your hand.
Destroy my impurities.
Sekhmet, Warrior, Beloved Goddess.
I call upon You now.

Light a bit of copal, dragonsblood, sandalwood, or frankincense, and smudge yourself with the smoke.

I stand in the breath of Sekhmet.
By Her blessing am I cleansed.
She purifies the uncertain heart.
She drives away despair.
She brings illumination.
Show me the way, please, Mother,
Beyond my ego, beyond my fear.
Show me the path to Your arms.

Light a red candle.

I stand in the light of Sekhmet.
By Her fire am I blessed.
May the burning flame of the Warrior
Guide me on my path today.
May my hands be Her hands,
My voice Her voice
And my actions pleasing to Her.
May every breath I take burn with devotion to Her.
Show me the way, my Warrior,
That I may taste of Your fire.

Anoint forehead with water, pomegranate juice, or red ochre, blended with sandalwood oil until it forms a paste.

I am bathed in the blood of Sekhmet.
May I never fear Her wisdom.
May I never fear the wisdom of the Warrior.
May I not cringe from Her expectations.
May I be strong.
May I be blessed with courage and an abundant heart this day.
Show me the way, Mighty Goddess,
That I may walk with integrity through the world.

Taste a bit of salt and then take a stone, any stone you associate with Her, and hold it in your hand. Mine is a simple black stone I found in the park on the day of my initiation. Spend at least ten minutes centering yourself with a four-fold breath: inhale four counts, hold four counts, exhale four counts, hold four counts.

I am rooted in the strength of Sekhmet.
May I be held securely in Her protection.
Hers is the will that destroys all obstacles.
Hers is the fierce power that banishes all entropy.
Show me the way, Great Lion of the Desert,
That I might, today at least

Conquer the vagaries of my own heart.

Bow and place your forehead on your altar before your statue of Sekhmet. Sit back and offer the following prayer:

Beloved Sekhmet,
I am Your temple.
Set me ablaze with Your light.
Fill me with Your fire's furious rapture
that I may dance unscathed
for Your delight.

Hail, Sekhmet. As I go forth this day, may I serve You well.

Offer thanks to the Goddess, extinguish the devotional candle, and go about your day.

Morning Ritual to Sekhmet and Ra
Kira R.

An altar to Sekhmet and Ra should be prepared and the sacred space consecrated. Priest/ess or Devotee offers the following invocation:

Homage to Thee, oh Great Sekhmet, from the swelling of Thy heart flame burst into being. Sublime Lady, most beloved in the face of the Sun, Whose fierce heat and warrior's heart drives back all opposition, thus earning Thee the name "Opener of the Way," descend upon us in all Thy brilliant glory.

As the Sun rises in the sleepy east, bestow upon us a parcel of Thy majestic strength that we may face this new day fearlessly as the lioness faces down her prey. Transform us in the conflagration of Thy fire that each dawn may bring us one step closer to Thee. Pre-eminent One in the Boat of Millons of Years, Scorching Eye of Ra, Whose diadem is infinity, awaken our hearts, allow Thy light to shine forth from our brows this day, that we may walk bathed in Thy grace.

Oh Mistress of the Heavens, come into this temple. Hail and welcome!

Priestess lights a candle and offers the following oracle, given by Sekhmet to Her priestess. If this ritual is being done alone, devotee should meditate either on these words or on Sekhmet's image.

Oracle of Sekhmet

Passion. Uncontrolled. I am raw passion. Invincible. Unyielding. You fools who deny your emotions deny Me. Vengeance, anger, hatred: I am all of these things. They are all my gifts. I do not seek sheep. I will not tolerate cowards. I am strength of body, mind and spirit. I am the Warrior Whose will formed the worlds. I do not cringe from power, neither should My children.

I am the flame that gives life to the Sun. I am the fire that burns away fear. Awaken. I will consume your fears in the inferno of My heart. I will make you fearless and strong, self-reliant as My children should be. *There is no wound so great that it can resist My healing flame.* I made You each in My image. I gave you souls of steel, each of you is tempered with My own heat, molded to My form. Be strong. Do not deny this precious gift, for in honoring your strength You honor me. Do not yield before adversity. Be fearless. Fear blackens the soul and desecrates the temple that is your body. My temple. Give your fear to Me. Live. Relish life. Burn with My flame.

Walk proudly, secure in My love. Do not run from my fierce claws. I will chase. Do not cower. I will rend. Do not grow arrogant in your skills or strength. I will destroy. Do not ignore Me or My power or I will consume you in My flames. Remember, I can devour the soul. Open your eyes. Bask in My fire and choose carefully that which strengthens the heart. I reward those who seek to grow. Justice is My crown, My warrior children. Walk in that shining light and hear My roar in your hearts. Use your fury, use your ferocity. Ride them and bend them to your will. I gave them as gifts, flame made flesh, not masters. Feel the heat of your passions and rejoice for it is My hot breath upon your soul.

Priestess or Devotee offers the following prayer:

Blessed art Thou, oh Incomparable Warrior, whose very glance holds back darkness. All the denizens of the Heavens sing praises of Thy shining countenance, Lady of All Powers. Eldest of Gods, Thy glance is terrible and doth drive back the serpent Apep making safe the passage of the Sunboat. From the brow of Thy Father Ra, Thou dost smite the wicked and bestow abundance on Thy devotees. Most Holy Mother in the Boat of Millions of Years, who was before the Gods were, bless us this day with Thy life-giving strength. Let us not cringe or bow before the stressful pressures of our daily toil, rather let us face the day with a lioness's pride and fearless courage. Hail to Thee, Mother of Power.

Offer incense.

I offer this incense to the Supreme Light of Heaven, Beloved Sekhmet Whose terrible flame is as eternal as Her Father. May I be blessed with Her gifts of courage and strength this day.

Priest/ess or Devotee offers the following invocation to Ra:

Hail to You, Oh Ra, at your rising. Your beauty shines in our eyes when our faces rise to greet the sunlight as we greet the world each day. You proceed at Your pleasure in the night-barge. Your heart is joyful with a fair wind in the day barge and we are blessed by your passage across the heavens.

All Your foes are overthrown, the stars and sky itself acclaim You. Hail to You, oh Ra, when You rise and when You set. How beautiful are Your risings and Your settings on the back of Your granddaughter Nuit. We praise You as You traverse the sky in contentment. Hail, Most Holy Self-created Lord and welcome. Come into our Temple and into our hearts, Mighty Ra.

Oracle of Ra through His priest/ess:

I am the Word. I am the Vision. I am the furnace of heat that devours the night. I do not hurry. I flow like water across the back of My Mother. Become to become in My becoming. I make everything sacred. I am power and will manifest and made action. I renew the earth and it is My golden caress that calls you from dreaming. I am eternal birth. I am passion made flesh.

I birth the dawn and the day, drawing you to consciousness with the power of My song. Tendrils of My golden hair stream like serpents across the weary night. I am ever-birthing, self-creating. I am the energy needed to create life. Mine is the universal seed. My flame devours flame and spits it up anew. Let my golden breath open your hearts. Raise your face to my light. Let Me sanctify your bodies. My warmth will heal your spirits, renew your strength. I am the Word made flesh, the flesh made light. In My body is eternal transformation, eternal birth. In your spirits lies a seedling of My light, unite with Me. Let it burst forth and blossom under My rays. Become to become in my becoming.

Priest/ess or devotee offers the following prayer:

Adoration until Thee, Who returns again and again as Lord of eternal becoming, Who crated Thyself from the wisp of a thought in the belly of the Sky. All beings praise Thee and receiveth They caresses with joy. Praise until Thee, Lord of Heaven, the Life, Health and Strength of the Gods who Adore Thee in Thy beautiful presence as Thy riseth in the Atet boat. Oh living Strength, Glorious Ra, now and forever may Thy name be praised.

Offer incense.

I offer incense to Thee, Oh glorious flame-drenched Lord. May I be blessed with Thy gifts of strength and inspiration and may these things guide me throughout this day. Hail to Thee, Oh Lord of Living Strength.

Blessing of the Elements:
On the altar let there be burning incense, at least two candles, a bowl of salt, water and a small vial of oil. Take the incense and asperge oneself with the smoke saying:

In the name or RA, Lord of the Sun, who traverses the heavens each day, may I be blessed with clarity of thought, insight and inspiration. Hail, Mighty Ra.

Take a candle, allowing its heat to bless one's face and countenance saying:

Divine Goddess of Victory, mighty Sekhmet, implacable warrior, cunning tactician, Goddess of strength, show me the path to victory this day. Let no obstacle that I may encounter crush my spirit but grant me the tenacious courage to endure and overcome. Hail Sekhmet.

Anoint your brow with the oil and take a sip of the blessed water saying:

In the name of Ra who brings life to all things, may I be graced this day with spiritual, mental, and physical renewal. Homage to Thee, Lord of the Sun.

Take a bit of salt and place it on your tongue and say:

Great Lady of the House of Life, Goddess of Healing, Goddess of Might, through Your wisdom may I transform the difficulties, hurts, and challenges of this day into sources of growth and change and strength. Hail to Thee, Gracious Sekhmet. May I receive the blessing of the Gods this day and in my works.

Devotee or priest/ess goes to the window where he or she can feel the rising sun warming him/herself. Let its power and heat fill you until you can see yourself standing in a nimbus of fire. Say: "I am a temple of Ra." Allow the heat-fire to strengthen and grow brighter. Say, "I am a temple of Sekhmet." Spend a few moments in contemplation.

Closing Prayer:

Most powerful Sekhmet, I thank Thee for this rite. I burn with Thy flame and exult in Thy countenance. Oh Sublime Mother, walk with me today and always. I give thanks.

Hail to Thee, Glorious Ra, Who brings rest to the night sky. Thy glory is magnificent, Thy beauty sublime. Oh ever self-creating Lord, make my soul like that of Osiris, may I be blessed with the power to ever create myself anew, in the face of any adversity. Hail to Thee, who shines more brightly than any star in the firmament of heaven.

Thanks are given to Sekhmet and Ra for this day, this rite and Their blessings.

Helpful Sources:

Awakening Osiris, Ellis, Normandi. Phanes Press, 1988.

Dea, Robertson, Olivia. Cesara Press, 1996.

Egyptian Book of the Dead, Budge, E. A. Wallis. Dover, 1967.

The Goddess Sekhmet, Masters, Robert. Llewellyn Publications, 1990.

Egyptian Book of the Dead, Faulkner, R., University of Texas Press, 1972.

Sekhmet's Day

From the Pagan Book of Hours

Color: Red
Element: Fire
Altar: Upon a red cloth set two torches, the figure of a lioness, and a clay pitcher of beer mixed with red fruit juice.
Offerings: Meat. Blood. Wrestle with the Beast Within.
Daily Meal: Beer. Meat from a hoofed animal. Barley.

Invocation to Sekhmet

Long, long ago, Ra Lord of the Sun
Was wroth with the people of the earth,
For their disrespect and their carelessness,
And his anger was so great
That he called forth into existence
The lioness goddess Sekhmet
As a manifestation of his wrath,
And he set her upon the people,
Intending her to eat a few of them
And teach them all a lesson.
And Sekhmet leaped upon them,
But she did not stop her destruction,
And after three days she had killed so many
That Ra begged her to stop, regretting his error,
But she refused, saying that there would be no end
To her appetite for blood and death.
So Ra had beer dyed red as blood, and spread it
Over the field of carnage, and she drank,
And fell asleep, and was enspelled.
And so we hail Sekhmet, for within each of us
Is the beast of wrath whom we must propitiate,
And never let run wild, lest it slay
All that we hold dear. Hail Sekhmet!

(All respond: "Hail Sekhmet!")
Be merciful to us, we who cower
In your shadow, and feel your footprints within us.
(All respond: "Have mercy upon us!")
And may your hunting be plentiful,
And all your days bright with sun.
(All respond: "Hail Queen of the Desert Sun!" Then the red beer is poured as a libation, and the torches are carried outside, where they are left to burn out.)

Uniting With The Solar Lion
Shin Cynikos

Before I begin this, I must first state that I am an independent practitioner. I subscribe to no set "tradition", temple, house, or self-proclaimed pharaoh or religious leader. I answer only to my gods, and myself. This meditation is one I perform when I wish to honor Sekhmet, or connect to her in sacred communication.

The Setting: This meditation is best performed either at early morning at the rising sun, or in the evening when the sun begins to set (or both). I tend to perform mine in the evening as the sun is setting, simply due to time and scheduling constraints. Best done where the sun can easily be viewed, either outside, or in a room with large windows (like a sun room or porch). As one of the Eyes of Ra, Sekhmet is a solar deity, and the sun is not only a manifestation of Ra, but a manifestation also of her power and influence on Earth. The rising and the setting sun are very symbolic and meaningful events in just about every tradition. Even to the most secular person, these daily events symbolize endings and beginnings. This is very important to keep in mind with how you would like to structure your ritual meditation, and what you may want to think about saying to the Lady when you begin your sequence.

The Materials: I'm a rather sparse person when it comes to materials, but I'll give the basics of what I use, and suggestions for elaboration. A cloth, for sitting on and/or placing offertory objects on. What I use is a large scrap of vintage male African lion hide, originally scavenged from an old taxidermy mount and acquired from a friend. I am an inveterate scavenger of natural history objects and dead animal bits, preferably vintage, secondhand, or antique, for ethics purposes. I have used this piece of hide as either a cloak/shawl, or a blanket to sit and meditate upon, and lay out various offerings to Sekhmet. The color should be the colors of the desert—golden hues, sandy colors, deep red. As with Set, the color red is sacred to Sekhmet.

Another important object I always have on hand is beer. You can just serve this straight out of the bottle. And please, no Miller Light or Bud. Sekhmet is a Lady with fine tastes; she likes nice brews, such as amber bocks, something with a nice red hue. Microbrews and gourmet beers are a definite must here. I've found that Dogfish Head's Midas Touch is a popular offering for many of my deities. Beer was actually a very important element in Sekhmet worship in the past. Large amounts of it were consumed ritually to imitate the drunkenness that cooled her wrath, she came close to destroying mankind. Along with beer, music was played to soothe and please her. During these annual festivals, special platforms, such as one found in Luxor called the "porch of drunkenness", were erected for people to collapse on during these festivals. Now, I am not suggesting one get completely shitfaced during this meditation (which would actually defeat the purpose), nor am I suggesting that those who abstain for a variety of reasons cannot worship her. Pomegranate juice was also a very frequent offering to her, which was mixed with the beer to imitate the look of blood, enticing her to drink it. Pomegranate juice is just as valid a beverage as beer in this case. You can also couple this with an image, icon, or representation of beer (such as a photo or empty bottle) if you feel it necessary to incorporate this aspect. Other consumables include meat, such as beef jerky (organic or otherwise more pricey; no cheap gas station knockoffs for her), bread, deep red juices, and spicy and fiery foods.

Incense is another option, which I sometimes use. I say "sometimes" because over the years, I have developed respiratory upsets, and it has resulted in me being less tolerant of incense (in addition, it aggravates my migraine symptoms, depending on the type used). However, I try to offer her incense as often as I am able, because it is something she enjoys, and generally I find myself sitting in areas that are open or otherwise with good ventilation (and besides, in this case, this time is her time, and I try to make as many sacrifices as I am able). I tend to use Mediterranean or Middle Eastern-style scents, such as amber, musk, frankincense, or myrrh. The incense I use with the greatest regularity is Kyphi, which you can find explained here at: http://www.ancientegyptonline.co.uk/kyphi.html. It was one of the main traditional incense blends in Ancient Egypt. This incense was used both for its medicinal as well as spiritual purposes, and makes a great offertory incense for the modern polytheist. By far the best blend I've found that most pleases the deities I work with is from the makers Lodestone and Lady's Mantle (http://www.lodestoneandladysmantle.com/). But again, your mileage may vary.

Other items that can be included are red candles, and images and depictions of the sun or solar activities. Also important are various objects depicting lions (preferably female lions), such as lion carvings/fetishes, photos, or even old relics like bones, claws, and scraps of fur. Especially in the case of the latter, be sure you acquire these from ethical sources. I tend to scavenge mine from old antique taxidermy mounts (when the hide deteriorates, the claws are the only hard bits left), or old Victorian displays. Make sure you investigate your sources. And of course, last and anything but least (in fact, this would be one of the most important components), a statue or representation of Sekhmet. If you lack a statue of her, you can substitute a lion statue, carving or other similar object that has been designated specifically as her stand-in (most statues and related objects were stand-ins for the deities they represented, until they became ritually inhabited, such as in the Opening of the Mouth Ceremony).

Preparation and Setup: Arrange all these items in a way you see fit, or rather, how you feel may please the Lady. Go by your instinct, and what you feel she may be telling you. Felines and feline-deities are very good at expressing their desires; it is important to keep your ears open to listen to them speak. (This feeds nicely into the topic of stillness, which I'll delve into in the next section.) I tend to place any offerings in front of the representation of Sekhmet, with the sun directly behind (either setting or rising, depending on your venue). Make sure the area you are setting up in is clean (ritual cleanliness was important in Ancient Egypt), and also free of any distractions (ringing phones, curious animals, relatives or neighbors, etc.). Make sure you are clean, clear-headed, relaxed, and in the right frame of mind. This time is her time, and time for you to commune with her. If you have any special jewelry or clothing you have dedicated to her or that you associate with her, wear it, but make sure it's clean and neat. Lions spend a very large amount of their time cleaning and grooming themselves, so make sure you do the same when it comes to setting up time for her.

If you are biologically female and experience your monthly cycle, don't worry too much about this biological event in relation to your Sekhmet meditation. As the Scarlet Lady, Sekhmet has a strong association with blood as well as with the female menstrual cycle. I am a pre-op female-to-male transman who still goes through the female cycle, and Sekhmet was very influential in helping me deal with this difficult monthly time, and working within the liminality of my gender in-betweenness. While we're on this topic, as a deity with a strong association with blood, modern practitioners may leave blood offerings to her. This sort of thing should not be done lightly, as this is a deep and intimate affair, and deities tend to take blood offerings quite seriously. This may be a start of a particularly deep bond. If you decide to do such a thing, please take all necessary precautions. Use sterile diabetic lancets (found at your local pharmacy) and alcohol swabs, and keep these offerings away from other people. There are many resources, online and in book-form, which discuss proper protocol for the leaving of blood offerings.

Initiating the Meditation Sequence: Everyone has their own way of starting a ritual or meditation sequence, as influenced by their personal practice or the group, temple, or organization they practice with. I tend to be very free-flowing with my ritual and meditation setups, going as the mood and spirit(s) strike me to. I tend to begin with some sort of percussive event, such as the clapping of hands or ringing of bells (Shinto practitioners are known for this sort of thing). This attracts the attention of attendant deities and spirits, and helps shift the brain into a mode conducive to ritual. I then light the combustibles, incense and/or candle. I place the food and drink before her image, or before the sun as it makes its way across the sky. If there are other offerings or objects you would like to dedicate to her, a prayer you would like to say, or a letter you've written to her (I tend to write letters to my deities on papyrus or paper, which I then ritually burn), now would be the time to offer it to her.

After the offerings have been laid out and presented, make sure you are sitting in a meditative pose. I tend to sit cross-legged on the floor, similar to the Lotus Position, or I kneel. Kneeling itself isn't just a submissive posture (something that those of us with Catholic upbringings may have programmed into our heads), but is also a posture of readiness and receptiveness. Lions sit in similar postures when scanning the savannah for suitable prey. If you like—and I do this frequently—lean forward and place the tips of your fingers or palms on the ground, and shift some of your weight onto them. This imitates a lion sitting upright in the grass, something I personally call the Lion Posture. This posture can work well for those, like myself, who work with and move lots of energy, and need a steady grounding source as they are moving and working along. But overall, pick a position that is comfortable to you, and one you won't fall asleep in.

Engage in a breathing exercise of your choice (my personal favorite is the Fourfold Breath). Utilizing diaphragmatic breathing (or belly-breathing) is very useful, as it enhances energy flow and allows for optimal metabolization of oxygen. This type of breathing (along with the reverse—Pre-Natal Breathing) is very useful for meditative purposes, and readying the body for energy work. Relax your muscles as you are breathing. I find that flexing each limb or portion of my body, starting from the feet up, helps. You may need to do this prior to assuming your favored meditative position.

The next step is entirely yours from here on out. I don't do guided meditations; I simply help set up the venue and allow for people to have their own experiences, independent of cued imagination exercises. Allow yourself to shift into an altered state. I tend to get a rushing sort of sensation, a swoop in the stomach, and/or tingling in the extremities. Focus on the sun (but don't stare directly *at* it). If any outside thoughts come barging in, don't focus on them, allow them to pass on through. Think about Sekhmet. Think about everything you associate with her. Think about her effect on your life. Talk to her. She is a very patient listener, but don't mistake this patience as complete acceptance. Sekhmet does not tolerate whiners, complaining, or excuses. If you have a problem, she will help you—but be prepared for the consequences. She comes from the School of Hard Knocks, and her influence may not always be a welcome occurrence at first. She is a goddess of destruction, and if necessary she won't hesitate to tear down your illusions, expectations, and harmful tendencies. Be prepared for sudden and potentially harsh change in your life if you go to her for help. But be honest with her, too. If you try to fib, she'll find you out quick, just as a lion picks out a sick or injured gazelle in a herd of hundreds.

Bringing It to a Close: Once you are finished communing with her, slowly bring yourself down out of the meditation in a way you see fit. Do not "dismiss" her; be polite and take your leave once you feel you are finished—and that she is finished with you, also. Be sure to thank her for the blessings she has bestowed on you, or the advice and inspiration she has given you. Take all the time you need. Ground as necessary. Stretch, and make sure your body is in working order. These meditations may last anywhere from minutes to hours, and you may either be very stiff, or a little too relaxed.

If you have consumable offerings (food, beer and/or juice), dispose of it in a respectful manner in accordance with your tradition or practice. I consume my offerings myself. Food is a precious thing, and the Ancient Egyptians, living in a comparatively harsh environment, understood this. Food was very frequently offered to the gods, then consumed by the priesthood and worshipping masses in ritual feasts and banquets in honor of said deity or deities. A modern interpretation would be that the gods consume the vital essences of the meal, and when we consume it with them it is considered a form of sacred communion. It is a very deep and intimate experience. I was also taught a particularly harsh lesson about the value of food by going through a period in my life where I went hungry involuntarily. As a result, I treat food, especially food offered to the gods, with much respect. Other options for offerings disposal are in a ritual fire (please practice appropriate fire safety and observe local laws), by leaving them in a body of water (be sure the food you are leaving will not somehow contaminate the waterways), or by a base of a tree or outside altar, to be returned to the elements. When it comes to beverages, I pour out some as a libation, and drink the rest myself.

Be sure when you clean up your space that you leave the area as you found it. This is especially the case if you happen to be meditating in an outdoor area, such as a park or other place utilized by the public.

Above all else, if you made any promises to Sekhmet, be sure to keep them. Show your gratitude, and don't let your offerings end when the ritual is over. There are many opportunities to donate your time or money to charities and causes in her honor. I will leave a list of resources below to consider. Donating time and money are great ways to cultivate your relationship to her in your life. Sekhmet is an amazing goddess. Union with her can be ecstatic, powerful, inspiring, beautiful, terrifying, exhilarating, or all of the above. Be prepared when approaching her. She is certainly not for the fainthearted. But once you stand in the presence of the Lion, be prepared to be forever changed.

For Further Research:

Sekhmet, Powerful One, Sun Goddess, Destructor by Caroline
    Seawright:
    http://www.touregypt.net/godsofegypt/sekhmet2.htm,
    retrieved September 25, 2010

Ancient Egypt: The Mythology —Sekhmet

    http://www.egyptianmyths.net/sekhmet.htm

Constantine, Storm and Coquio, Eloise. *Bast and Sekhmet: Eyes of
    Ra.* Robert Hale Limited, 2006

Meeks, Dimitri. *Daily Life of the Egyptian Gods.* Cornell University
    Press, September 1996

Naydler, Jeremy. *Shamanic Wisdom of the Pyramid Texts: The
    Mystical Tradition of Ancient Egypt.* Inner Traditions,
    December 9, 2004

For Offerings of Time and/or Money:

USO, http://www.uso.org, retrieved September 25, 2010

Soldier's Angels: http://www.soldiersangels.org/, retrieved
    September 25, 2010

Sekhmet is a warrior goddess, and to honor her it is important to honor and take care of those that serve in the military. I am offering resources for American service personnel, because that is my home country. Please get in touch with your local veterans' organization or political figure for information on supporting those in the armed services in your home country.

AfriCat: http://www.africat.org/, retrieved September 25, 2010

Big Cat Rescue, http://www.bigcatrescue.org, retrieved September 25, 2010

Kavita Lion Lodge: http://www.kavitalion.com, retrieved September 25, 2010

As a feline goddess, it is greatly important that we protect and conserve Africa's big cats (as well as big cats all over the world). With their territories shrinking fast due to human activity and poaching, many are endangered or nearing extinction. You honor her by honoring and protecting her sacred manifestations here on Earth.

Keeping An Altar To Sekhmet
Kira R.

I have maintained a small altar shrine for Sekhmet for many years, ever since I first began honoring Her. I began doing this because it seemed like a good idea, and it was strongly suggested to me by my teacher and mentors. I didn't realize that it would become a powerful learning process, and one of the primary ways by which I learned, however slowly, to show proper respect for the Gods.

When I first started keeping Her altar, it sort of felt like playing house. I had an image of Sekhmet seated, an offering bowl, incense holder, a few lion's teeth and claws in a bowl, a big piece of tiger's eye, which I associate with Her, and a clay vase for flowers. I also had a small rattle with the design of a lion wood burned on it and some feathers. I would move things around, light incense, bring flowers, offerings, pray and keep it clean, but for the first year or so I really had no true connection with what I was doing. It was a ritual to be done because this was what I had undertaken to do. There wasn't, as yet, any connection. I hadn't learned to be properly mindful.

I don't know when that changed. One day, though, it "clicked". One day, I realized that I wasn't just following the motions, I wasn't just moving things around as a corollary to my prayers. I was making space for Sekhmet in my heart, in my life, in the deepest recesses of my soul. Working my altar, as I was wont to do, was a conscious, living symbol of that process. It was an invocation, an invitation, and unconditional welcome. Tending the altar rapidly became a metaphor for tending my soul and my devotional relationship with Sekhmet. It became a powerful outward expression of that internal reality.

I learned that devotion takes work. That it takes mindfulness and ongoing attention. It can't be left to molder; it will not tend itself. I learned that with a very little bit of daily effort (just like regularly dusting the altar and changing offerings), I could keep my spiritual connections open and healthy. I learned to love this process of engagement. I learned to love this one gentle path by which one might approach Sekhmet. I learned that offerings and rituals didn't have to be elaborate and complex to be effective; that the real mystery of connection lies in the time and consistency of effort that one might choose to give.

I like how my altar became central to my home. It served and serves as a visible, visual reminder of the Divine nexus around which my world revolves: Sekhmet. It serves as a reminder that it is up to me to welcome Her blessings and wisdom into my life. No one else is going to do it for me.

Slowly, with the grace and blessings of Sekhmet, I learned. I learned respect and the protocols of respectful engagement. I learned to better love and serve Sekhmet. That is no small thing at all and in many ways, it all began with my maintaining a shrine.

Tips to Keeping a Good Altar

❖ Give it a central place in your home, somewhere where you will have to look at it regularly, whether or not you are thinking about engagement.

❖ Keep it clean. It's so disrespectful to allow an altar to accrue dust, or to become disordered and untidy. I have found that the way one's altar looks is often an extension of the way one maintains one's spiritual life.

❖ Keep the altar active. It's not enough to keep it clean; use it. Try to spend some time there every day. Incorporate it into your devotional work as a place to pray, meditate, talk to Sekhmet, make offerings. Try to make offerings regularly. I do so at least once a week, usually on Saturdays.

❖ Keep it pretty. In addition to everything else, I use my altar as a visual representation of my relationship with Sekhmet. Over the years it's grown a lot from the small shelf with a statue and handful of trinkets and bowls to space that takes up an entire wall. It is a mandala and "medicine" space, marking the depth and richness of my relationship with this Goddess. It reflects many years of devotional work.

❖ Finally, be consistent. I don't think it matters what you do, so long as you keep on doing it and doing it respectfully. It is a Goddess that you're dealing with, after all.

May Sekhmet open our hearts to devotion.

Sekhmet's Ritual Objects
Galina Krasskova

(These are drawn from observation and twenty-plus years of devotion to Sekhmet. Your mileage of course may vary, and I encourage folks to experiment and not to reject an offering or item because it doesn't appear here. Use this as a very subjective guide.)

Colors: Red, orange, yellow, gold –the colors of fire and the desert sun.

Symbols: The lion/ess, fire.

Altar Suggestions: Blades, lion's teeth/claws, pomegranates, tiger's eye, carnelians, garnets, red, orange, yellow flowers, sand, images of lions and other big cats, candles, oil lamps (any sort of fire), feathers to represent the feather of Ma'at, solar images, the ankh, ancient surgeon's tools (She does have a path as a Goddess of healing, after all), weapons of all sorts.

Food and Drink: Pomegranate juice/wine, good dark beer, fresh meat, various hard liquors, cinnamon schnapps.

Service Offerings: Study a martial art as a form of devotional work to Her, donate to Doctors without Borders, American Friends of Kenya (www.afkinc.org), or a comparable organization. Donate to an organization dedicated to saving big cats.

Contraindicated: Hubris, moral cowardice, willful weakness of spirit, fleeing one's spiritual or community duties, passive-aggressive behavior of any sort, emotional incontinence or inability to deal effectively with one's own anger.

Recipes

Sekhmet Blessing Oil
Galina Krasskova

In a base of sweet almond oil, blend the following:

❖ 40 drops dark musk
❖ 40 drops civet oil
❖ 10 drops patchouli
❖ A few drops of your own blood

It goes without saying that this oil should only be used for the person making it. If you intend to use this for other people, omit the blood and add seven pomegranate seeds instead.

Sekhmet Oil
Galina Krasskova

In a base of sweet almond oil, blend the following:

❖ 20 drops myrrh oil
❖ 20 drops frankincense oil
❖ 25 drops civet oil
❖ Seven crushed cardamom seeds
❖ A pinch of dragonsblood
❖ 7 pomegranate seeds

Blend together and allow to sit in the sun for seven days before using.

Sekhmet Incense
Jason Freysson

Combine equal parts of the following:

- ❖ Catnip
- ❖ Patchouli (oil and herb—put several drops of the oil on the herb and allow to dry. It enhances the smell)
- ❖ Musk root (*ferula sumbul*)
- ❖ Civet oil carried by heather (put the oil on dried heather flowers and allow to dry)
- ❖ Dragonsblood
- ❖ Bay
- ❖ Balm of Gilead
- ❖ Cascarilla
- ❖ Aloe
- ❖ Jalap
- ❖ Valerian
- ❖ Spikenard
- ❖ Rue
- ❖ Cascara sagrada
- ❖ Life everlasting
- ❖ Sandalwood
- ❖ Frankincense
- ❖ Lotus
- ❖ Cinnamon
- ❖ Benzoin (powder and oil)
- ❖ Jasmine (flower and oil)

This emphasizes warriorship, courage, and sexual energy, all of which Sekhmet possesses in abundance. Blend the ingredients together thoroughly. I use a blender to make sure I have a nice, fine grain. A base of sandalwood and copal may be used.

Bread For Sekhmet

Branglas

This recipe was produced as a collaboration between Sekhmet and myself. I used my knowledge of historical cooking, and she made her personal preferences clear in a polite but firm manner, which is why the dates are not left in whole pieces as I originally planned, and also why the measurements are expressed in the more accurate weights and precise fluid measures rather than in cups.

Egyptian bread was renowned for its quality throughout the Classical World. Part of the reason for its famed lightness was the Egyptian beer brewing industry—fermenting beer makes an excellent leavening agent, producing a better and faster rise than the sourdough leavens that were used in Mediterranean countries. For those raised on modern baguettes and supermarket white bread, it may seem unlikely that the moist, cake-like bread that this recipe produces could be considered exceptionally light and delicate. Having experimented with a number of ancient bread recipes, I can assure you that compared to unleavened barley cakes and to the wine-based Roman sourdough (ancient sourdough technique did not at all resemble the very complex, multi-stage process that has been developed for modern artisanal sourdough), this Egyptian bread is a miracle of sweet, fluffy lightness. Since both sweetness and lightness were difficult to achieve and expensive until comparatively recently, this is also a fairly high-status bread, suitable for offering to a goddess, while still having enough substance and flavour to make it acceptable to Sekhmet personally. The enrichment of the dough with egg and oil would also have made this more of a festival than an everyday bread.

If you happen to have access to a vat of fermenting beer, then substitute that for the beer and dried yeast in the recipe below. Judging by my own experience, rising times for the dough should not be substantially affected. Skim your beer off the top of the vat, making sure that you get plenty of the yeasty foam. If you do use fermenting homebrew, when heating it with the honey and dates make sure it never gets warmer than blood-heat, otherwise the yeast will be damaged.

We know from tomb paintings and archaeological finds that Egyptian bread was baked in small clay moulds. If you wish to approximate this, use small, brand-new, clean and well-greased terracotta flower pots. Put a bit of foil in the base to cover the drainage holes and place the pots upright on a baking tray with crumpled foil between and around them if support is needed. The baking time required will be shorter than that given below.

Even the finest of ancient flours were not as fine as modern, commercially produced white flour. I have chosen to use plain commercial wholemeal, which is still several steps above the flour used by Egyptian peasants, as modern wholemeal does not usually contain spiky bits of chaff and stem along with a generous sprinkling of fine gravel from the grinding process. If you wish to use something more like a very high-status, fine Egyptian flour, sift the wholemeal through a sieve to remove the heaviest part of the bran before measuring.

The flavour of the finished bread is heavily dependent on the beer and oil that you use. I developed this recipe with a dark, British-style stout and used locally produced extra-virgin olive oil. The result was a dark bread, with a pronounced, complex flavour that had a bit of a bittersweet edge. If you want a paler and milder bread, use a milder brew (lager was *not* approved of) and regular, mild oil. I was going to suggest that you could also increase the amount of honey by another tablespoon, but that was decidedly frowned on, so I can't recommend it. Put it down to the complications of developing recipes under deity guidance. For historical authenticity, strictly speaking, the beer used should be ale, made without hops, rather than modern hopped beer. However, ale is difficult to get commercially and Sekhmet didn't seem to mind the substitution (when I say "didn't seem to mind", I mean "downed what was left in the bottle with every sign of enjoyment").

The Recipe:

- ❖ 12oz wholemeal flour
- ❖ Small saucepan
- ❖ 200ml beer
- ❖ Wooden spoon
- ❖ 1 large egg
- ❖ 9x5 inch loaf tin (internal measurement)
- ❖ 4oz dates, finely chopped or minced
- ❖ Medium-sized casserole dish
- ❖ 50ml olive oil
- ❖ Large mixing bowl
- ❖ 5ml (1 tsp) salt
- ❖ Sharp knife and chopping board
- ❖ 5ml (1 tsp) dried yeast
- ❖ 30ml (2 tbsp) honey
- ❖ Boiling water

Put the beer, honey, and chopped or minced dates into a small saucepan and simmer, stirring constantly with a wooden spoon, until the honey is melted and the pieces of date are broken up and separated. Never leave beer unattended while heating as it can easily bubble up and boil over. Put it aside to cool to lukewarm.

While the beer mixture is cooling, put 4oz of flour into a large mixing bowl and stir in the dried yeast. Add the lukewarm beer mixture to the flour and yeast and stir well; this is your sponge. Cover and set aside at room temperature for 2-3 hours. At the end of that time the sponge should be about doubled in volume and full of bubbles and air. If you're patient enough, you should be able to watch bubbles slowly forming and collapsing at the surface of the mix.

Add the salt, oil, and egg to the sponge and stir thoroughly until everything is well mixed in. Mix in the remainder of the flour. The finished dough will be very wet, too wet to knead conventionally, but apparently the ancient Egyptians did work with fairly wet doughs that were mixed with a hoe, rather than kneaded in the more modern fashion. Cover the bowl with plastic wrap and place in the fridge overnight (about 12-14 hours).

The next morning, take the dough out of the fridge and leave it to come to room temperature, one to two hours. While the dough is warming, grease and flour the loaf tin. You can also line the loaf tin with baking paper, but this will not give such a neat appearance when the loaf is removed. When the dough is ready, wet your hands with water and knead lightly to deflate it, then tip into the loaf tin and spread as evenly as possible. Pre-heat the oven to 200 °C (400 °F). Cover the dough and leave for about an hour in a warm place until it's risen to about two-thirds of the way up the tin, and is spongy but still has a little springiness.

Just before putting the bread into the pre-heated oven, fill the casserole dish about half-way with boiling water and place it on the shelf below the bread. Bake the bread for about 30 minutes, until the loaf is well-risen, brown on top, and you can lift it out of the pan easily without it breaking. A fully-baked loaf should look dry on the surface and sound hollow when tapped on the bottom. Cool on a wire rack. This bread keeps well and I can testify that slices left on a bread-board overnight with only a tea-towel over them were still perfectly moist and edible the next morning. It should have good "altar-life".

Ideally, bread should never be cut until it's fully cooled. Cutting the loaf while still warm will result in a heavier texture and cause the bread to go stale more quickly. Having said that, the first time I made this I found that I suddenly became extremely hungry while the test loaf was still in the oven. I ended up feeling compelled to break my own rules and cut the end off the loaf almost as soon as I put it on the cooling rack. The steam from the hot bread was judged a satisfactory offering and I found the warm, buttered bread very tasty. Perhaps, if baking this as an offering, it might be a good idea to make it in the small flower-pots, or in miniature loaf tins, and then break a couple of the mini loaves apart and offer them while they're still warm.

Sekhmet Libation Offering
Ana Anpuhemet

This is a simple libation recipe I have used on several occasions for Sekhmet. This recipe stems from the legend of Sekhmet as the Wrath of Ra. You may have heard the legend that Ra had sent Sekhmet to destroy the evil-doers on Earth, but Her bloodlust became so great that she slaughtered, without prejudice, the guilty and the innocent. Her bloodlust was so great that the Gods were worried that the Mighty One would wipe out humankind, and the wise God Tehuti (Thoth) made a plan to subdue Sekhmet. He directed that a concoction of beer and pomegranate juice be made, which was then glamoured to taste like blood. This mixture was spilled a field in Sekhmet's path. When She came upon it, She lapped it up, thinking it was blood, and She was calmed by a drunken slumber, thus ending Her rampage and the immediate threat to humankind. This is my version of that drink for Sekhmet.

Through the various research I've done regarding ancient beers, it appears the closest to ancient beer is an extra stout form. I tend to gravitate toward Guiness Extra Stout beer. There are brands available in limited supply of more authentic recipes—one such is Pharaoh's Brew—as well as numerous recipes online of how to make your own replica of ancient beer if you are the adventurous brewing type.

Thankfully, due to the modern marvels of grocery stores, pomegranate juice is readily available year-round and can usually be found in the fruits and veggies section. I tend to use the brand Pom since it is the most popular, but any pure pomegranate juice will suffice.

The number seven for the droplets of blood comes from the legend where it is said seven barrels of this mixture was made for Sekhmet. In offering blood, there is no need to be careless. I have a diabetic lancing device to draw my blood. Please make sure you do not share the lancets with others, always use a clean lancet even though you are the only one using the pen, and swab the area on your skin where you are going to draw blood with a rubbing alcohol wipe. All of these items can be found in your local pharmacy.

I usually mix this in a large container and pour into a dedicated cup.

Closing Prayer
Galina Krasskova

May Sekhmet be hailed.
All praise and adoration be given to Her.
It is Her due,
and our joy to give.

May those who love Her
learn at Her feet,
the majesty of Her wisdom,
the overwhelming grace of Her fire.
May we learn to reverence Her,
properly.

To honor Her is a blessing.
To hear Her name a joy.

Hail Sekhmet.

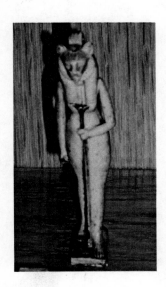

CPSIA information can be obtained at www.ICGtesting.com
Printed in the USA
LVOW131022240413

330707LV00001B/26/P